c50

Arkansas

A Bicentennial History

Harry S. Ashmore

W. W. Norton & Company, Inc.
New York

American Association for State and Local History
Nashville

Copyright © 1978
American Association for State and Local History
All rights reserved

Library of Congress Cataloguing-in-Publication Data

Ashmore, Harry S.
  Arkansas, a Bicentennial history.

  (The States and the Nation series)
  1. Arkansas—History. I. Title. II. Series.
F411.A85   976.7   77–26622
ISBN 0–393–05669–4

Published and distributed by W. W. Norton & Company, Inc.
500 Fifth Avenue
New York, New York 10036

Printed in the United States of America

1 2 3 4 5 6 7 8 9 0

For Hugh B. Patterson, Jr.

Contents

Illustrations

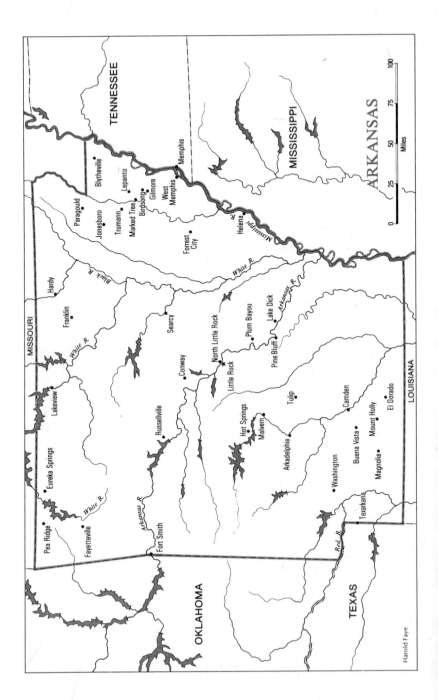

Harold Faye

Invitation to the Reader

IN 1807, former President John Adams argued that a complete history of the American Revolution could not be written until the history of change in each state was known, because the principles of the Revolution were as various as the states that went through it. Two hundred years after the Declaration of Independence, the American nation has spread over a continent and beyond. The states have grown in number from thirteen to fifty. And democratic principles have been interpreted differently in every one of them.

We therefore invite you to consider that the history of your state may have more to do with the bicentennial review of the American Revolution than does the story of Bunker Hill or Valley Forge. The Revolution has continued as Americans extended liberty and democracy over a vast territory. John Adams was right: the states are part of that story, and the story is incomplete without an account of their diversity.

The Declaration of Independence stressed life, liberty, and the pursuit of happiness; accordingly, it shattered the notion of holding new territories in the subordinate status of colonies. The Northwest Ordinance of 1787 set forth a procedure for new states to enter the Union on an equal footing with the old. The Federal Constitution shortly confirmed this novel means of building a nation out of equal states. The step-by-step process through which territories have achieved self-government and national representation is among the most important of the Founding Fathers' legacies.

The method of state-making reconciled the ancient conflict between liberty and empire, resulting in what Thomas Jefferson called an empire for liberty. The system has worked and remains unaltered, despite enormous changes that have taken place in the nation. The country's extent and variety now surpass anything the patriots of '76 could likely have imagined. The United States has changed from an agrarian republic into a highly industrial and urban democracy, from a fledgling nation into a major world power. As Oliver Wendell Holmes remarked in 1920, the creators of the nation could not have seen completely how it and its constitution and its states would develop. Any meaningful review in the bicentennial era must consider what the country has become, as well as what it was.

The new nation of equal states took as its motto *E Pluribus Unum*—"out of many, one." But just as many peoples have become Americans without complete loss of ethnic and cultural identities, so have the states retained differences of character. Some have been superficial, expressed in stereotyped images— big, boastful Texas, "sophisticated" New York, "hillbilly" Arkansas. Other differences have been more real, sometimes instructively, sometimes amusingly; democracy has embraced Huey Long's Louisiana, bilingual New Mexico, unicameral Nebraska, and a Texas that once taxed fortunetellers and spawned politicians called "Woodpecker Republicans" and "Skunk Democrats." Some differences have been profound, as when South Carolina secessionists led other states out of the Union in opposition to abolitionists in Massachusetts and Ohio. The result was a bitter Civil War.

The Revolution's first shots may have sounded in Lexington and Concord; but fights over what democracy should mean and who should have independence have erupted from Pennsylvania's Gettysburg to the "Bleeding Kansas" of John Brown, from the Alamo in Texas to the Indian battles at Montana's Little Bighorn. Utah Mormons have known the strain of isolation; Hawaiians at Pearl Harbor, the terror of attack; Georgians during Sherman's march, the sadness of defeat and devastation. Each state's experience differs instructively; each adds understanding to the whole.

The purpose of this series of books is to make that kind of understanding accessible, in a way that will last in value far beyond the bicentennial fireworks. The series offers a volume on every state, plus the District of Columbia—fifty-one, in all. Each book contains, besides the text, a view of the state through eyes other than the author's—a "photographer's essay," in which a skilled photographer presents his own personal perceptions of the state's contemporary flavor.

We have asked authors not for comprehensive chronicles, nor for research monographs or new data for scholars. Bibliographies and footnotes are minimal. We have asked each author for a summing up—interpretive, sensitive, thoughtful, individual, even personal—of what seems significant about his or her state's history. What distinguishes it? What has mattered about it, to its own people and to the rest of the nation? What has it come to now?

To interpret the states in all their variety, we have sought a variety of backgrounds in authors themselves and have encouraged variety in the approaches they take. They have in common only these things: historical knowledge, writing skill, and strong personal feelings about a particular state. Each has wide latitude for the use of the short space. And if each succeeds, it will be by offering you, in your capacity as a *citizen* of a state *and* of a nation, stimulating insights to test against your own.

James Morton Smith
General Editor

Introduction

WHEN I made up my mind to go west and pursue my fortune in Arkansas I was, like so many who had preceded me, resident in that lovely stretch of country at the base of the Appalachians where blue and smoky mountains angle across from Virginia to Georgia. I would be, I knew, following a worn trail. In the course of the nineteenth-century expansion of the Cotton Kingdom a third of the population of North Carolina crossed over the ridge, and two-fifths of the residents of my native South Carolina.

Most of these came from within a few hundred miles of Charlotte, the metropolis of the Carolina upcountry where I was then situated as editor of the evening *News*. This Piedmont belt provided the first resting place for the eighteenth-century migrants called Scotch-Irish. There, along with their Highland cousins, yeomen from elsewhere in the more or less United Kingdom, and a handful of nonconformist Germans, the tough-fibered men and women from Ulster staked out the first American frontier. Their imprint made this a domain distinct from the haughty colonial outpost of empire established in the low country by the assigns of British lords proprietor. This was, above all, protestant country, in politics as well as religion.

In the Waxhaws just down the way a gangling boy named Andrew Jackson fought the British and came to Salisbury to read law before going on to Tennessee to put his fierce stamp on a new era of American politics. A little to the west and south, some thirty miles from where I was born and reared, Old Hickory's mortal enemy of the same blood, John C. Calhoun, built an austere mansion at Fort Hill; there he set forth the philosophical underpinning for a great slave empire. The years had done little to change the essential composition of the upcountry population; Charlotte was reputed to be the only major city in the United States where Presbyterians were in a majority, or, for all practical purposes, seemed to be; and it was duly noted that the largest single alphabetical classification in the phone book was to be found under MAC—SEE ALSO MC.

So it was that I took with me to Arkansas an inherited folk wisdom. The look and speech of the people there would not fall strangely upon my eye and ear, and, given time, I would be able to establish cousinhood with many; yet I knew too that, while this would not diminish their hospitality, and might enhance it, I would be something of an interloper to those who got there first.

It was my conceit that I had improved upon my natural equipment by seeking knowledge of the whole of the southern region. As a fledgling political reporter assigned to the South Carolina capital at Columbia I had become aware of the parochial limits of my formal education. In 1941 a Nieman Fellowship at Harvard gave me access to that institution's considerable faculty, and I concentrated with Paul H. Buck, a leading authority on the southern Reconstruction, Frederick Merk, the historian of the westward movement, and the pungent analyst of American manners and morals, the elder Arthur Schlesinger. These studies were interrupted by a summons to service with the infantry in the European theater of operations. A stint under arms was practically foreordained for one of my ancestry, and it formed another bond with the Arkansans, who have been disproportionately represented in every citizen's army the nation has mustered since 1846, when the new state provided the staging area for the Mexican War.

When I assumed the editorial chair at the *News* I understood that the job called for a professional southerner—not one of those who respond with a literary rebel yell to any fancied slight to the honor of Dixie, but one who could apply his ingrained sense of the region's unique character to the effort to determine where the South might be going. This was not a task for one likely to be diverted by an impulse toward moral recrimination; my predecessor had been W. J. Cash, author of *The Mind of the South,* and his presence at the *News* had survived his passing.

At Charlotte I was in the orbit of Chapel Hill, where the leading regional prophet, Howard Odum, had assembled an outstanding company of social diagnosticians. So I would find myself comparing notes with the likes of Alexander Heard, now the chancellor of Vanderbilt, then apprenticed to V. O. Key in preparation of *Southern Politics*. And if I wanted a more diverting, but no less discerning view of the new South emerging from the dislocations of World War II there were long evenings of poker with an expatriate New Yorker who had founded a shoestring publication called the *Carolina Israelite*. His name was Harry Golden.

In due course I attracted the attention of J. N. Heiskell, proprietor of the *Arkansas Gazette*. He was one of the last survivors of the once-familiar breed who could qualify under Marse Henry Watterson's specifications for a successful editor, being endowed with learning, wisdom, sensitivity, courage—and 51 percent of the newspaper's stock. At seventy-five, Mr. J. N. professed a need to be relieved of some of his duties, a premature judgment as it turned out, since he lived to be a hundred and continued to show up at the office almost until the end.

Mr. J. N. was himself something of a historian, or at least an antiquarian, who had begun collecting Arkansiana soon after he arrived from his native Tennessee in 1902 upon his family's purchase of the *Gazette*. The curator of that remarkable residue, Margaret Ross, has observed that its most severe limitation results from the proprietor's assumption that anything he could remember couldn't properly be construed as history, so that any incidental relics of his own long tenure were likely to be relegated to the newspaper's morgue. Working with Mr. J. N. was a constant reminder that journalism and history are part of the same running stream.

There was another credential for a senior editorial appointment, with which, fortunately, I had been equipped at birth. At the time I joined the remarkable company already assembled there the *Gazette* was the most consistently Democratic newspaper in what was then the most consistently Democratic state in the Union. I come of what I like to call an old political family, which also has been referred to in its native habitat as a courthouse ring. The result was that I could hardly be challenged at the portals of the great one-party edifice which now sheltered an uneasy alliance of Bourbon conservatives, rambunctious heirs of the antiestablishment Populists, romantic mourners of the Lost Cause, and social engineers of the New Deal.

In my first election year at the *Gazette*, 1948, I took the occasion of our morning editorial conference to remind Mr. J. N. that we had not yet formally endorsed the national presidential slate, and that many of our nominally Democratic competitors had declared for Thomas E. Dewey. He had reservations about Harry Truman, he said, but of course we would support the ticket. I had the temerity to inquire whether the *Gazette* had ever been anything other than Democratic. He peered out of his permanently open office door to be sure he couldn't be overheard and replied, "I don't like to talk about this, but the fact is we went Whig twice." This anecdote has long since earned a place among the journalistic apocrypha that attend the memory of one who lived so long and indulged so sly and deceptive a wit. But it belongs here, too, I think, since it served as comeuppance to a newcomer subject to the arrogance common to those who grew up in one of the first-born seaboard states. It was J. N. Heiskell's way of reminding me that Arkansas, and the *Gazette*, had been around for a very long time.

Some of the things I knew, or thought I knew, stood up fairly well in broad stroke. Arkansas, like all the southern states, is divided into upcountry and low, and there is a historic conflict of political and economic interest between those who live in the hill country to the north and west and the owners of the rich lands in the south and east. The plantation belt follows the alluvial plain and the river valleys, and some of the nation's largest individual agricultural holdings are located there. From the beginning it has supported an authentic landed gentry, few in number but long on influence. Until recent years the planters, in combination with the business and professional men in the one principal city, Little Rock, and the lesser towns, dominated the state most of the time—but there has not been a season since the Civil War when they have been immune to challenge from those who spoke for, or claimed to speak for, the majority of Arkansans of lesser means.

In many ways Arkansas seemed to me not only to be typically southern, but even more so. In this century the state had known the greatest outmigration and the least inmigration of all those that gave their allegiance to the Confederacy; the result had been to prolong and preserve the cultural stagnation that submerged the whole of the South in the post–Civil War period. The plantations made the transition from slavery to sharecropping without any profound change of character, and in the hills subsistence farming continued to deplete the thin soil and in time to drive the surplus population to the west, where they acquired notoriety as the Arkies of the depression years. In the statistical accounting, from income to education, Arkansas ranked near the bottom of the list of states; at the chamber of commerce the census reports provided only an occasion to thank God for Mississippi.

But I soon came to sense a difference. In the Carolina of my youth there were those who still spoke quaint near-Chaucerian English and sang Elizabethan ballads, but in those mountain coves there was a profound sense of looking back to a lost and forgotten time. I could hear the same inflections and sounds in the Ozarks, and in the uncertain light from a cabin fireplace it would be hard to say that these lean and shambling mountaineers were any different from the ones back home. But here there was a feeling of frontier, of still unrealized history.

So it is with accent. In Arkansas I heard then, and still hear, the whole southern range from magnolia soft to mountain burr. But there is something distinctive, an emphasis that sets off Arkansas speech whether it echoes the Deep South intonations of Mississippi on the east, or the aggressive address of the Texans to the west. The style can, I suppose, be described as self-deprecating, but there is no whining overtone of self-pity; when explaining their special ways to strangers, Arkansans sound to the practiced ear as though they are resigned to dealing with fools, but are too polite to say so.

Brooks Hays, the former congressman who has earned a place as one of the state's great raconteurs, says that as long as he can remember he has heard of the Arkansan traveling abroad who always replied to anyone who asked where he was from: "Arkansas. Go ahead and laugh." Some Arkansans with inflated pretensions and thin skins resent the backwoods stereotype that has been saddled upon them since the nation first laughed at the colloquy between the uncouth squatter and the Arkansas Traveler. But most understood that the grizzled native invented the joke, and made the Traveler its butt. With good reason Vance Randolph, the Ozark folklorist, titled one of his collections *We Always Lie to Strangers*.

Arkansans, like all southerners, also have had occasion to deceive themselves. The plantation system that pushed back the Indians at the beginning of the last century depended upon black slaves, and Arkansas entered the Union in 1836 in a political trade-off with free Michigan. There were those among the new state's leaders who privately recognized that slavery was, at best, a necessary evil, but publicly there was no effective dissent from John C. Calhoun's thesis that human bondage was a positive good. That notion prevailed, not only among the few whose economic well-being depended upon forced black labor, but among the great majority who owned no slaves and were themselves victims of the concentration of the state's wealth and political energy in the service of a single special interest. The heritage that survived the lost Civil War was a political theology based on white supremacy, and this prevailed even in areas where Arkansans sided with the Union and fought in blue uniforms. In lily-white mountain counties signs appeared warning hapless black transients not to let the sun set on them.

Yet it was always true that the ritual professions of bigotry were not matched by prevailing practice. Blacks knew, of their own experience, that behind the monolithic rhetorical facade there was a wide range of personal relationships among blacks and whites, embracing love and compassion as well as insensate cruelty. Shared history and common culture provided the saving grace when Arkansas, along with the rest of the South, was forced to recast its social institutions to make a new accommodation for the black minority.

It had been obvious since the end of World War II that time was running out for the legal and extralegal barriers of racial segregation; if whites still professed to be unwilling to accept blacks as equals, blacks were making it clear that they would no longer accept anything less. And so, somewhere, the showdown had to come. It turned out to be at Little Rock.

In the year before the Supreme Court's *Brown* decision outlawing segregation in public education, I headed a task force of some fifty southern scholars assembled by the Fund for the Advancement of Education to establish the dimensions of the region's dual school system and consider what might follow if the court held it had to be merged or reconstituted. Somewhere along the way I ran into an old Arkansas politician who asked me what I was up to. I told him I was about to publish a book under the title, *The Negro and the Schools.* "Son," he said, "you have got yourself into the position of a man running for sonofabitch without opposition." In the stormy times to come there were many to accord me, and the *Gazette,* the fate reserved for bearers of bad news. I would have occasion to be grateful to the founder, William E. Woodruff, who as far back as 1820 prudently declared against dueling as a matter of principle, thereby relieving the editor of any moral obligation to defend his honor against a challenge to mortal combat.

And the news was very bad, serving to concentrate the flickering attention of the national media upon a city and a state most of its representatives had difficulty locating on the map. The hit-and-run journalism of the electronic age makes its points with stereotypes, and these were quickly fashioned to fit the desegregation crisis at Little Rock. Gov. Orval Faubus qualified for the role of villain when he seized Central High School with National Guard troops to defy a federal court order requiring the admission of nine black children. A visiting reporter required to encapsulate his commentary on the sound track of three minutes of filmed mob action could hardly treat with the subtleties of a wily hillbilly motivated not by racism but by political expediency; and the drama that builds TV audiences would be discounted if it were pointed out that what was being wrought before the cameras was not incipient revolution, but a kind of diversionary confusion.

So the complex Little Rock story was presented to the world as a black-and-white morality play. Worst of all, the media treated the historic confrontation as though it were an event that began and would end in Arkansas—missing the critical point that the race issue was no longer rooted in the peculiar institutions of the moribund Confederacy, but had become intertwined with all our basic national policies. That perception also eluded Dwight D. Eisenhower, who did nothing to prepare the nation for the predictable consequences of the Supreme Court's recasting of the nation's racial policy. When the president by his silence denied southern moderates the moral support of his office, only the site of the confrontation remained in doubt. The practical consequence was that the general found himself with no means to counter the defiance of the governor of Arkansas except to invoke the ghosts of Reconstruction by sending in the United States Army.

In the course of these events I became something of a stereotype myself, experiencing the peculiar frustration that comes of being at once praised and blamed for the wrong reasons. And this, I think, gave me new insight into the special quality of the Arkansas character. Deep in the Arkansas consciousness is a tragic sense that across nearly three centuries of existence as colony, territory, and state its people have been misunderstood and put upon.

Until very recent years Arkansas's most valuable export has been its sons and daughters. They turn up everywhere, in high places and low. When *Forbes Magazine* published its 1976 list of highest-paid American business executives, eleven native Arkansans were near the top, running such enterprises as airlines, hotel chains, steel mills, and department stores. One who goes to Yale seeking the Sterling Professor of History finds C. Vann Woodward of Vanndale. The sweet singer, Glen Campbell, is one of the good old Arkansas boys. They brought Martha Mitchell home for burial at Pine Bluff. When Eldridge Cleaver emerged in the red glare of a Black Panther shootout in Oakland I was not surprised to find that he was born in Little Rock, or to discover that the distinguished poet, Maya Angelou, was raised by an indomitable black grandmother at Stamps, down in Lafayette County.

All of these migrants took away with them something of Arkansas, as did this more-or-less adopted son when I resumed the westward trek, settling finally at the end of the historic trail on the Pacific Coast.

Looking back from this western perspective I see remarkable

change—what I suspect could be the most dramatic transformation taking place in any state of the Union. For generations Arkansans have been streaming off the land, displaced by the mechanization of agriculture. Now the process is complete. The familiar sharecroppers' shacks have disappeared or stand empty in the fields; the plantations have become agribusinesses, where corporate managers and a few skilled technicians employ machines and chemicals in place of hand labor; sloping land where patch farmers' fought a losing battle with erosion has become green pasture supporting a major beef cattle operation; in 1976 soybeans, chickens, and rice ranked ahead of cotton as money crops.

Little Rock has exploded in the usual American pattern; downtown became a place of parking lots and high-rise office buildings as urban sprawl continued to bulldoze its way into the wooded hills; in 1976 the city voted to annex another fifty-five square miles. But the clutter has not yet eliminated a pervasive sense of the land. In the cold black of an early winter morning there is still the sound of automobiles starting up along quiet suburban streets, signalling the exodus of a small army of business and professional men setting out to meet the dawn in the duckblinds. Most will bag the limit and be back in town by nine.

The natural beauty of the state has been greatly enhanced by the belated development of its river systems. The fickle Arkansas, which scourged the countryside with floods and shrank to a trickle in seasons of drought, now runs bank-full the year around, controlled by locks and dams that open navigation far back into what used to be Indian country. The quality of life has visibly improved for those who stayed behind when the rural population thinned out. The process has left only ghosts in the smaller villages, but there is a new vitality in the surviving towns.

A few years ago the migratory flow reversed, and now expatriate Arkansans, white and black, are coming home—along with a swelling tide of outlanders attracted by the state's pastoral pleasures. When social scientists and community leaders gathered in 1976 for a conference on Ozark inmigration at the old resort town of Eureka Springs, most of those present were not gratified, but appalled, by the Census Bureau's report that the mountain counties were experiencing the highest growth rate of any nonurban area in the nation, and could double their population in eight years.

So the long curve of history runs. My assignment is to appraise the main currents that have brought Arkansas to this pass. It will be seen that the work is colored by affection for those who have lived there, and for some of those who still do. It may be objected that I am attempting to meet in limited compass the requirement I heard voiced in South Carolina many years ago: what we need is a good, objective history of the South written from the Confederate point of view. And already the opposite suspicion has arisen. When the *Gazette* announced that I would undertake the bicentennial summing up, my old antagonist, the sometime supreme court justice and segregationist leader, Jim Johnson, dispatched a letter to the editor objecting that this was akin to retaining Benedict Arnold to write the history of the American Revolution. Justice Jim wrote in great good humor, and knew I would so receive his message. It was a splendidly Arkansan welcome home.

HARRY S. ASHMORE

December 1977

Arkansas

1

Boundaries for a Game Preserve

$\mathcal{T}$HE place called Arkansas always had as its eastern boundary the great, meandering Mississippi River, a barrier for those traveling east and west, and a means of passage for voyagers coming down from the north. Mountain ranges provided a natural demarcation to the north and west, and in the south there was bayou country. The first occupants of the 53,104-square-mile trapezoid to emerge clearly from the mists of prehistory were identified as Akansa, or "downstream people," by their relatives among the Illinois tribes. They settled along the west bank of the Mississippi and the lower reaches of the 1,500-mile tributary that still bears their name, embellished by orthographic additions as the original French rendering passed into English.

In the last third of its course eastward from the Continental Divide the Arkansas River bisects what originally was a vast game preserve. Forest cover ran from the mountains to the alluvial flatlands in the south, broken only by the low-lying Grand Prairie in the east. Fresh-flowing streams cut easy passage for men and animals through rugged terrain, and abundant rainfall and mild winters provided forage for the grazing herds of the midcontinent and the migratory waterfowl of the Mississippi flyway.

Buffalo, elk, and deer roamed the valleys; black bear were numerous along the steep, regular ridges that rise abruptly a hundred and fifty miles upstream from the mouth of the Arkan-

3

sas; turkey and quail drummed in the underbrush, clouds of chattering Carolina parakeet were a common sight, and there were flights of ducks, geese, and passenger pigeons so dense they dimmed the sun; game fish shared clear mountain streams with a population of beaver and otter, and huge alligator gar slid through the still waters that laced the lowlands; and everywhere in the woods there were predators, wolves, foxes, weasels, and the big cats who under various names—cougar, mountain lion, panther, painter—shared the bounty with the aborigines.

The first white men to intrude upon this Stone Age Eden pulled up short on the east bank of the Mississippi on May 21, 1541. They traveled in the company of Hernando de Soto, already two years away from his base in Cuba. Under orders of the king of Spain to explore the interior of Florida, he had plunged on into the uncharted area subsequently to be designated Georgia, the Carolinas, Tennessee, Alabama, and Mississippi. It had been a rough journey. Encounters with the Indians and the elements had cost the expedition at least two hundred dead, a third of its horses, and most of its baggage. Rodrigo Ranjel, the commandant's secretary, left a description of the arrival at the Father of Waters that stands in sharp contrast to the romantic painting often reproduced to depict that historic moment:

> I saw a gentleman, called Don Antonio de Osoria . . . with a jacket made of the skins and martens of that country, all broken at the sides. His flesh showed through. He had no hat; was barefoot and without breeches; a buckler at his shoulder, girt with a sword without a sheath; and thus he marched in all the frost and cold. He endured his toil without laments, such as many others made, for there was no one to help him, although he had in Spain two thousand ducats of income through the church. And the day I saw him he had not eaten a mouthful; and if he wished to sup, he had to dig the earth with his nails to get something to eat.[1]

De Soto set his bedraggled conquistadors to work constructing four large barges, a task complicated by the necessity of dodging volleys of arrows dispatched by canoe-borne Indians

1. John Gould Fletcher, *Arkansas* (Chapel Hill: University of North Carolina Press, 1947), p. 11.

ranging the mile-wide river. A month later the Spaniards came ashore in Arkansas, probably at Sunflower Landing below the present town of Helena. De Soto's force mustered four hundred men, something less than two hundred horses, and a drove of hogs that served as an ambulant commissary—and, legend has it, as the founding stock for Arkansas's razorbacks.

For the next year de Soto and his men moved among the Indians, sometimes doing battle with them, sometimes enjoying their hospitality, in either case taking what they needed, including slaves. While there is some quibbling over details, those who have attempted to reconstruct the expedition's log generally agree that the Spaniards went north to the Saint Francis River country, looped south to the valley of the Arkansas, turned upriver to the beginning of the Ozark mountains, angled west into the Ouachitas, then marched southeast into what is now Louisiana. There de Soto died, before he reached the open water that took the remnants of the expedition across the Gulf to Mexico.

The surviving records provide only a sketchy glimpse of the great Indian nations of the transmississippi as they experienced this first encounter with the outriders of an alien culture. The conquistadors paid their epoch's highest compliment to the Caddo, whom they encountered in the Ouachitas, citing them as the best fighting men they came upon in all their arduous passage. Although the de Soto expedition left no trace on the land, not even a Spanish place name, this passing exchange between white and red men foreshadowed the course of events that would shape the history of Arkansas.

More than a century went by before men with pale faces again set foot on the west bank of the lower Mississippi. In 1673 two Frenchmen and five Indians came floating down the great river after setting forth from Mackinac at the head of Lake Michigan. The Jesuit priest Jacques Marquette had been assigned by the king's intendant to accompany the fur trader and geographer Louis Jolliet in an effort to determine where the waterway emptied into the sea. Jolliet must have seen ample employment for his commercial talents by the time the two pirogues reached the mouth of the Arkansas. There the voyagers ended their expedition, heeding the warning of friendly Indians that they were entering territory where they would be subject to capture by hostile tribes under Spanish influence.

Nine years later René Robert Cavelier, Sieur de la Salle, set out from Canada with a party of fifty-four, including Indian women and children. Pausing to raise a cross bearing the arms of France in the area where Marquette and Jolliet had turned back, he continued downriver to the Gulf. There on April 9, 1682, he proclaimed the whole of the Mississippi Valley the French territory of Louisiana, so named in honor of Louis XIV.

Henri de Tonti, a Sicilian officer who had been la Salle's second in command, came back in June 1686 in a futile search for his leader, missing in the course of an ill-starred expedition from France that had run aground on the shore of what is now Texas. Heading north again de Tonti stopped off to claim the land grant promised for his service to King Louis, leaving behind a handful of his compatriots on a tract at the confluence of the Arkansas and White rivers a few miles inland from the Mississippi. This was the genesis of Arkansas Post, which survived to open the fur trade in the interior and provide those traveling under French protection a haven midway between Illinois and the Gulf. It was the first white settlement in the lower Mississippi Valley, predating New Orleans and Natchez by more than three decades.

De Tonti's choice of the site no doubt was determined by the amiable disposition of the Akansa, who maintained their villages in a loose confederation given the tribal designation Quapaw. He had recorded his first, favorable impression when the la Salle expedition put in at the mouth of the Arkansas on March 13, 1682. De Tonti wrote in his journal: "We were well treated and given a cabin for our stay. . . . It can be said these savages were the best of all we had ever seen. They had fish in abundance, roosters and chickens, and several kinds of unknown fruits." [2]

This co-operative spirit continued undiminished among the Quapaw, enabling the French to keep the fleur-de-lis flying at

2. Works Progress Administration, *Arkansas: A Guide to the State* (New York: Hastings House, 1941), p. 35.

Arkansas Post with a garrison of a few soldiers and the ministrations of an occasional visiting priest. The notion that the vast expanse of fertile land that lay beyond might produce something more valuable than the furs brought out by itinerant *coureurs de bois* was first taken seriously in 1717, when John Law sold the French Government the development scheme that came to be known as the "Mississippi Bubble." The Scot promoter projected an initial settlement of six thousand white Europeans and three thousand African slaves.

Law staked out his own duchy of some twenty-five hundred square miles in the area around Arkansas Post, and advertised its charms by quoting a euphoric description of the Quapaw by le Page du Pratz: "The beauty of the climate has a great influence on the character of the inhabitants, who are at the same time very gentle and very brave. They have ever had an enviable friendship for the French uninfluenced thereto either by fear or views of interest; and live with them as brethren rather than neighbors." [3] Most of those who responded were brought down by epidemics suffered in transit and never completed the ocean crossing. During 1720 and 1721 the vanguard, mostly recruited in the Palatinate, arrived at Biloxi to pick up slaves from Guinea. Before they could settle at Arkansas Post, however, the Mississippi Bubble burst and Law fled France. The disillusioned colonists—perhaps a hundred in all—headed downriver for New Orleans to seek passage home. Louisiana's first governor, Jean Baptiste le Moyne, Sieur de Bienville, persuaded them to resettle in an area above New Orleans still known as the German coast.

The collapse of John Law's scheme left at Arkansas Post a residue of forty-seven settlers, described in 1722 by the explorer Benard de la Harpe as living in badly situated cabins and virtually devoid of the means of subsistence. The effort to exploit the area's agricultural potential would not be resumed for a hundred years, but the French now recognized that development of the port of New Orleans endowed the little outpost with mili-

3. Thomas Nuttall, *Journal of Travels in the Arkansas Territory During the Year 1819* (Philadelphia: Thomas Palmer, 1821), p. 83.

tary significance. Pierre Francois Xavier de Charlevoix wrote in a 1721 Arkansas Post entry in his *Journal of a Voyage to North America:* "Our alliances with the Illinois has set us at variance with the Chicahuas [Chickasaw] and the English of Carolina blow up the dissention. Our settlement in Louisiana is a great eyesore to the Spanish as it is a barrier which we have placed between their powerful colonies in North America and Mexico; and we must expect they will employ every method in their power to destroy it." [4]

For the remainder of the century Arkansas Post was little more than a dot on the maps of the global strategists. Father Paul de Poisson, dispatched from New Orleans in 1727 to assure the settlers that the district had not been abandoned, reported a French population of thirty. A census in 1744 recorded twenty white soldiers and ten black slaves. In 1770 the British Capt. Phillip Pittman described the post as a stockade situated about three leagues from the mouth of the Arkansas: ". . . the sides of the interior polygon are about 180 feet, and one three-pounder is mounted in the flanks and faces of each bastion. . . . The Fort stands about two hundred yards from the water-side and is garrisoned by a captain, a lieutenant, and thirty French soldiers, including sergeants and corporals. There are eight houses without the fort, occupied by as many families. . . . These people subsist mostly by hunting, and every season send to New Orleans great quantities of bear's oil, tallow, salted buffalo meat, and a few skins." [5]

The stockade was christened Fort Carlos III, and the French garrison then served under the flag of Spain. In 1762 the turn of events in Europe had forced the French to suspend their long struggle for control of the interior of the North American Continent; the treaty ending the Seven Years War also terminated the remote operations identified in American history books as the French and Indian War. In the settlement France ceded to Spain all territory west of the Mississippi, plus New Orleans and its enclave on the east bank.

In 1783 Arkansas Post experienced a major Indian attack, a

4. Margaret Ross, "Chronicles of Arkansas," *Arkansas Gazette,* April 8, 1960.
5. *Arkansas: A Guide to the State,* p. 358.

raid in strength by Chickasaw braves crossing the Mississippi from their ancestral domain. Thomas Hutchins, an American geographer who visited the post in 1784, reported ten killed, and Jacobo Dubreuil, the commandant, noted that he was required to buy a cask of brandy to revive the garrison. Dubreuil thought the British might be stirring up their Indian allies as prelude to an effort to annex territory west of the Mississippi to replace that lost to the American revolutionaries in the East.

No such campaign ever materialized, but the commandant's suspicion that some alien agency must have been involved is understandable. For a hundred years this isolated outpost maintained the French claim to a vast territory by virtue of the protection accorded the garrison by Indians who could have put it out of commission any time they were seized by a passing fit of choler. Captain Pittman estimated the strength of the "Arcansas or Quapas" in three villages near the post at six hundred warriors, and added: "They are reckoned among the bravest of the Southern Indians; they hunt little more than for their common subsistence, and are generally at war with the nations to the west of them." [6]

In 1800 a shift in the European power balance restored to France the Spanish holdings in the Mississippi Valley. Three years later the Emperor Napoleon and President Thomas Jefferson agreed on the Louisiana Purchase, conveying to the shaky American confederation lands that ultimately would comprise all or part of thirteen new United States. Military considerations, complicated as always by domestic political pressures, moved Jefferson to negotiate with the first consul.

There were now enough Americans west of the Appalachians to generate a significant commercial traffic on the river systems that bore their rafts and keelboats down to the port of New Orleans. In 1795 Spain had entered into the Treaty of San Lorenzo, authorizing the "Kaintucks" to pass goods through the mouth of the Mississippi without payment of duty, and to hold them there on deposit while awaiting transhipment. In 1802, presumably at the bidding of Napoleon, Spain suspended

6. *Arkansas: A Guide to the State,* p. 358.

the right of deposit, touching off a belligerent protest movement throughout the western territories. Jefferson at the same time was receiving alarming reports that Napoleon had plans to displace the accommodating Spanish, restore New Orleans to direct French control, and re-establish his hegemony in the hinterland. The president wrote to Robert R. Livingston, his minister in Paris: "The day that France takes possession of New Orleans we must marry ourselves to the British fleet and nation." [7]

Aside from heading off the prospect of undoing the Revolution, Jefferson had no way of knowing what else he got in return for the payment of $27,267,622 in cash and pledges agreed to in negotiations concluded in Paris on May 2, 1803. The machinations of the crowned heads left little doubt that, in legal terms, Napoleon conveyed a clouded title, and strict constructionists of the new United States Constitution argued that Jefferson had exceeded his authority in acquiring it. But there was no denying the strategic importance of establishing the American presence beyond the Mississippi, and so the deal held up.

In the spring of 1804 Lt. James B. Many of the United States Army ran up the Stars and Stripes at Arkansas Post. William Dunbar and Dr. George Hunter were dispatched from Natchez to ascend the Red and Ouachita rivers. An expedition led by Lt. Zebulon Pike headed west from Saint Louis, and at Great Bend in what is now Kansas detached a party under Lt. James B. Wilkinson to descend the Arkansas River by canoe. Wilkinson encountered a fur trader and a few French hunters, but passed no settlement en route to Arkansas Post. There was no reason to question the 1799 census of the Spanish commandant, who had reported 368 white residents in the Arkansas District.

In the forests that stretched away from the river banks, however, there was a shifting and increasingly agitated Indian population. Toward the end of the century tribes east of the Mississippi, responding to the pressure of white settlers pushing in behind them, began to range across the great river. Some of

7. John Fleming, *The Louisiana Purchase: From Wilderness to Empire* (Little Rock: Gallinule Society Publishing Company, 1972), p. 12.

these established permanent settlements in the domain of the Quapaw and the Caddo in the south. From the north there was an incursion by the militant Osage, who spread out in all directions from their hereditary lands in what is now Missouri.

William Dunbar, in his report to President Jefferson, described the Osage as "a lawless gang of robbers making war on the whole world." [8] They had, however, established a territorial claim with the Spanish commandant at Arkansas Post, who had given them permission to hunt along the Arkansas above the Canadian River. To complicate matters, the powerful Cherokee had crossed over from Tennessee to establish themselves north of the Arkansas. As early as 1785 small parties were hunting along the Saint Francis and White rivers, and ten years later the tribe made formal application for permission to settle permanently. They were turned down by the Quapaw, who were overruled by the Spanish. The Americans sanctioned this arrangement when they assumed jurisdiction over the disputed territory.

Under the act of March 26, 1804, providing for governance of the transmississippi, the resident tribes were treated as sovereign nations with recognized territorial hegemony. But the incoming white Americans significantly altered the previous relationship with the Indians, replacing the freewheeling French fur traders with a government "factory" to handle the exchange of goods for furs. Each of the tribes was assigned a resident agent, nominally a civilian, although most were former army officers and all functioned under the jurisdiction of the War Department.

Washington's representative to the Arkansas Cherokee was Maj. William L. Lovely, an elderly Virginian who had been assistant to the Cherokee agent in Tennessee. Taking up residence in an abandoned Osage village upriver from Little Rock, he described his situation in an old soldier's lament written in 1815 to a family friend, President James Madison:

> My situation is I can assure you disagreeable living at upwards of three hundred miles from a post office no ways of procuring information but those which are owing to chance and those seldom happen. So I may say with propriety that I am entirely secluded

8. Grant Foreman, *Indians and Pioneers* (Norman: University of Oklahoma Press, 1936), p. 22.

from the land of the living surrounded on all sides by Indians
together with the worst of White Settlers living just below me
betwixt whom there are daily disturbances arising and against whom
there are no possible means in my power of enforcing any laws.[9]

There was no longer any foreign enemy, actual or impending,
against whom the Indians could serve as useful allies; the Spanish settlements far to the south and west posed no real threat,
and the War of 1812 had effectively ended the possibility of
British intervention from Canada in the north. To the white men
now arriving in Arkansas in a swelling tide the Indians were
simply in the way. ''Banditi'' was the term Major Lovely used
for the first of these to make contact with his Cherokee charges.
The settlers heading west along the Ohio River water route and
overland around the base of the Appalachians were only in-
cidentally interested in trade with the natives; their goal was
possession of choice parcels of the land the tribes held under
treaty guarantee of the government that encouraged the immigration.

By 1815 there were sizable settlements in the New Madrid
area in what is now northeast Arkansas, and homesteads were
being carved out of the forests along the navigable rivers. The
land office in Washington, recognizing the urgent need for real
estate plats, sent out two deputy land surveyors to determine the
initial point from which measurements could be taken. Joseph
C. Brown headed west from the mouth of the Saint Francis
River, while P. K. Robbins proceeded north from the mouth of
the Arkansas. In the middle of a swamp near present-day
Marianna, Robbins's Fifth Principal Meridian intersected
Brown's base line, and from that point all surveys in Arkansas,
Missouri, Iowa, Minnesota, North Dakota, and part of South
Dakota take their initial bearing. The monument erected by the
Daughters of the American Revolution ignores the intrepid sur-
veyors but duly records the political compulsion that brought
them there: ''This stone marks the base established November
10, 1815, from which the lands of the Louisiana Purchase were
surveyed by United States engineers. The first survey from this

9. Foreman, *Indians and Pioneers,* footnote, pp. 34, 35.

point was made to satisfy the claims of the soldiers of the War of 1812 with land bounties.''

Volunteers for the war with Britain had been promised a tract of 160 acres in the Louisiana Purchase upon honorable discharge, and if a veteran chose not to homestead his land the title was transferable and could be sold for cash. Many found themselves at loose ends in New Orleans, where the troops were mustered out after Andrew Jackson's successful campaign marked the end of hostilities. These, along with a horde of sutlers and assorted camp followers, saw opportunity beckoning along the Arkansas and Red rivers. The operations of these footloose entrepreneurs among the Indians were characterized by Major Lovely as ''plunder in the first degree.'' [10]

The matter of establishing the boundaries of the purchase also was taking on urgency. The agents of the contracting parties hadn't been much help. On May 20, 1803, Livingston wrote to Secretary of State Madison to report on his negotiation with Napoleon's representative, Talleyrand. Unable to elicit any specific limits to the territory ceded by Spain to France and in turn to the United States, Livingston asked if the Americans were to construe it their own way. Talleyrand replied: ''I can give you no directions; you have made a noble bargain for yourselves, and I suppose you will make the most of it.'' [11]

In 1819 when the United States purchased directly from Spain disputed territory in east Florida, the negotiations provided an occasion for boundary settlements with both Spain and Britain. In the south, Spanish Texas was set off by the Sabine and Red rivers with some arbitrary connections in between. In the far west the Arkansas River was used as a marker under what amounted to a gentlemen's agreement, since no one then knew where its headwaters rose. The British agreed to establish the boundary with Canada at the 49th parallel.

In this process Arkansas began to take on fixed dimensions of its own. First designated as a district of Louisiana, jurisdiction was then vested in Indiana Territory until 1812, when Congress

10. Foreman, *Indians and Pioneers*, p. 137.
11. Fleming, *The Louisiana Purchase*, p. 20.

established Missouri Territory, whose legislature created Arkansas County to embrace a nonaboriginal population recorded
in the 1810 census as 1,062. By 1818 increasing immigration
had prompted the Missouri Legislature to subdivide the original
county, adding four: Lawrence, Pulaski, Clark, and Hempstead.

Missouri was now pressing for statehood, and the Arkansans
in their turn were petitioning Congress for territorial status. On
March 2, 1819, President James Monroe signed the act creating
the Territory of Arkansas. The eastern border was still the great
river. The northern and southern boundaries were straight lines
laid out with a ruler, except for a northeast corner nipped off by
influential landowners who wanted to remain citizens of Missouri, and a section in the southwest where the arbitrary border
with Louisiana ran into a loop of the Red River setting off
Texas under the treaty with Spain.

There was no fixed dividing line to the west. The great plains
were still terra incognita, the domain of vast herds of buffalo
and the mounted Indians who followed their migration with the
succession of the seasons. The animals provided food, raiment,
and fuel for the fierce plains tribes who exercised militant sovereignty over hunting grounds extending all the way from the Rio
Grande to the upper reaches of the Missouri. For decades to
come the great hairy tide and its outriders provided a barrier to
colonial expansion beyond Arkansas's western mountains.

2

"Peace by Eternal Bribes"

ALTHOUGH he never doubted the wisdom and practical necessity of the Louisiana Purchase, Thomas Jefferson recognized that true title to the vast lands lay, not with the self-appointed French sovereign who deeded them to him, but with the aborigines who had lived there time out of mind. A product of the first frontier, the Virginian understood that to the Indians war was an honored vocation, and he was not disturbed by the fact that they often had been allied with the nation's enemies. In 1791 he offered a pragmatic formula for dealing with the problem: "The most economical as well as the most humane conduct toward them is to bribe them into peace, and to retain them in peace by eternal bribes." In 1808, when Gov. Meriwether Lewis of Louisiana Territory was having trouble with the Osage in the Arkansas District, Jefferson advised economic sanctions: "Commerce is the great engine by which we are to coerce them and not war." [1]

If this formula called for a prodigious swindle, it at least was intended to avoid the indiscriminate slaughter and inhuman treatment permitted and sometimes encouraged by Jefferson's successors. As political power shifted from the seaboard across the Appalachians to the thrusting new communities of the second frontier, Indian rights were no longer a moral abstraction but a

---

1. Fawn M. Brodie, *Thomas Jefferson: An Intimate History* (New York: Bantam Books, 1975), p. 106.

15

palpable barrier to the ambitions of land-hungry whites. The demand of the frontiersmen was for the most expeditious removal of the tribes from areas they held under the protection of the federal government. On their side, the Indians could only see in the advancing tide of settlers a threat of extinction.

In Arkansas the indigenous tribes had developed a stable village culture, with a considerable agriculture, but they remained dependent on game brought in from the surrounding forest. Their concern was not with a given tract of land, which was in any case communal, but with control of the extensive hunting territory required to sustain the tribe. Until they began to appear in numbers sufficient to be deemed threatening, white strangers usually were greeted hospitably. The *coureurs de bois,* whose trade of manufactured goods for furs occasioned the first departure from the Indians' subsistence economy, moved freely among them and often settled down long enough to found mixed-breed families. That situation changed drastically with the advent of white men whose stated purpose was to clear the land and drive off the game.

Yet, despite a great deal of individual violence, there was never anything approximating sustained warfare between red and white men in Arkansas. Across the years when the interests of the two races were diametrically opposed there was sustained intercourse in all the forms to which the term may be applied. Southerners, whose leaders tried to erect an absolute barrier of law and social sanction against miscegenation with blacks, had no such compunction about the Indians. If whites who took Indian mates were looked down upon in some quarters they were never placed wholly beyond the social pale. There were mixed breeds among the most prominent tribal leaders, and these bore the patronyms of proud southern families—Ross, Chisholm, McIntosh, Douglas, LeFlore, Pickens. As president, Jefferson openly commended racial intermingling as the ultimate solution of the Indian problem, saying to a group of Delaware, Mohican, and Monrie who called on him in 1808: "You will mix with us by marriage, your blood will run in our veins, and will spread with us over this great island." [2]

2. Brodie, *Thomas Jefferson,* p. 587.

These contradictory attitudes were reflected in the careers of the two great southerners who were primarily responsible for the national policies that determined the development of Arkansas Territory as it progressed toward statehood. Although one is enshrined as an urbane, even haughty patrician, while the other symbolizes the dawning era of the common man, John C. Calhoun and Andrew Jackson grew up within a hundred miles of each other in upcountry South Carolina, and came from the common Scotch-Irish stock. There were elders in the families of each who could tell at first hand of pitched battles with the Cherokee.

Calhoun, appointed secretary of war in 1817, was charged with evolving federal procedures to secure and develop the transmississippi; Jackson, as commanding general of the Southern Department, was responsible for executing the edicts of Washington in Arkansas Territory. Calhoun, attempting to hold to the humane Jeffersonian policy, soon found himself on collision course with the rough-and-ready border captain, and their personal differences would grow into one of the famous blood feuds in American political history. On the day after he left the White House in 1837 Jackson was asked if his eight years in Washington left him with any regrets. He said he had two—that he had been unable to shoot Henry Clay or to hang John C. Calhoun.

Calhoun created an Indian superintendency to bring together the previously unco-ordinated activities charged to the War Department. These involved the treaty relationship with the tribes carried on through Indian agents and the territorial governors, the function of the frontier army garrisons responsible for maintaining order, and federally regulated trade under the "factory" system.

In 1818 Calhoun proposed to Congress a comprehensive new Indian policy designed to meet new conditions. In the Missouri and Arkansas area he judged that it was time to move toward incorporating the Indians into the larger society. Here the tribes had been acculturated to the point where they could no longer be considered independent, free nations. Calhoun thought their only hope of survival lay in merger into the white community. He proposed that the government-operated "factories" be used to encourage agricultural pursuits to replace hunting as animals became scarce. To that end the Indians were to be established on lands of their own, with a guarantee against further demands for territory. This, he believed, would imbue in them the concept of individual property rights, while the annuities paid under existing treaties would go to educate their children, looking to their ultimate admission to citizenship with full political rights.

Congress took no action on Calhoun's proposal, and, as his biographer Charles M. Wiltse noted, more than fifty years went by before any significant part of it became law: "In the West men believed they had a divine right to fill Indians with whiskey preparatory to bargaining for their furs, and to kill a suitable number of braves every now and then as proof of the inherent superiority of the white man." [3]

When Arkansas achieved territorial status on July 4, 1819, the population, exclusive of Indians, had passed 14,000. A few settled families from the French period remained, and in time would be absorbed into the emerging frontier society. Veterans of the War of 1812 now were arriving in force, and among the old soldiers was the territory's first governor.

"Brigadier General James Miller has accepted the appointment of Governor of this territory," the *Arkansas Gazette* reported in its first issue, November 20, 1819. "He is probably now on his way, and may be expected here as soon as the water rises." In an adjacent column was a communication signed by "A Citizen of the Territory" presaging the troubles that lay in wait for the new administration. The agitated subscriber recounted the efforts of Governor McMinn of Tennessee to arrange the removal of the whole of the Cherokee Nation from his state to the Arkansas River country, and warned: "Fellow-citizens, suffer me to call your most serious attention to this open, public and official declaration of hostilities against your country, your property, your rights, your freedom, your laws, your liberty, and your lives!" [4]

The proconsul dispatched from Washington to take charge of

3. Charles M. Wiltse, *John C. Calhoun, Nationalist* (Indianapolis: Bobbs-Merrill Company, 1944), p. 156.

4. *Arkansas Gazette*, Nov. 20, 1819.

this fermenting frontier turned out to be something less than an ideal choice. James Miller was an authentic hero, a New Hampshire man who had served with distinction as colonel of the Twenty-First Connecticut Volunteers. In 1814, at the battle of Lundy's Lane in upstate New York, he responded with, "I'll try, sir!" when ordered to take a British battery, and boldly moved forward to do so. The battle was inconclusive, but Miller came out of it with a gold medal voted by Congress, a brigadier's star, and a place near the head of the line when the government began distributing transmississippi plums to the veterans of the confused conflict.

The general did what he could to impress his new constituents with the majesty of his federal commission. In September he arrived at Pittsburgh, where the government had waiting a keelboat for his river journey to Arkansas Post. This ordinarily humble craft was fitted with a capacious, handsomely furnished deck cabin, the name "Arkansaw" emblazoned in gold letters on both sides. The flagstaff above the cabin flew a large banner bearing the slogan, "I'll try, sir!" Miller, in company with some twenty relatives and friends and a cargo of munitions for the territorial militia, made a leisurely journey down the Ohio and Mississippi, docking at Arkansas Post the day after Christmas.

The floating symbol of national sovereignty seems to have made little impression upon the newly anointed citizens of Arkansas Territory. It may be assumed that the territorial capital had a similar effect upon a proper New Englander. In his *Journal of Travels in the Arkansas Territory During the Year 1819,* the most discerning observer of the period, the Philadelphia botanist Thomas Nuttall, described Arkansas Post as an

> infant settlement of the poor and improvident. . . . Nature has done so much and man so little [Arkansas Post] after existence of near a century scarcely deserved geographical notice, and will never probably flatter the industry of the French emigrants, whose habits, at least those of the Canadians, are generally opposed to improvement and regular industry.[5]

5. Thomas Nuttall, *Journal of Travels in the Arkansas Territory During the Year 1819* (Philadelphia: Thomas Palmer, 1821), pp. 107, 109.

A proper concern for the dignity of his position would have been sufficient to deter Governor Miller from participating in the usual social life of the community, which Nuttall found to consist primarily of dram-drinking, contests of physical strength, and gambling.

Indian trouble was waiting for the new governor. On June 20, 1820, he reported to Secretary of War Calhoun that the Osage under Chief Mad Buffalo had fallen upon a Cherokee hunting party and killed three braves. This was ominous but not unusual news from the area north of the Arkansas. Two years before, the War Department had established its westernmost garrison three hundred miles upstream from Arkansas Post, and Calhoun now suggested to its commanding officer, Maj. William Bradford, that he enlist Miller as mediator. The governor dawdled, and it was not until December that arrangements were made for a peace conference.

General Miller and the Cherokee chiefs showed up at Bradford's headquarters at Fort Smith but the Osage didn't. So Miller and Bradford led a column of troops west to the Verdigris River for a parley with Mad Buffalo. The Yankee general obtained what he considered reasonable terms of settlement, but when he returned to present them to the Cherokee he ran into a militant chief whose prestige matched his stubbornness. An eyewitness described the confrontation: "[Miller] would have succeeded except for the influence of Ta-kah-to-kuh. His uniform answer to all arguments for peace, whether urged by Cherokees or by agents of the United States government, was, 'The Osages are liars, and no liar should ever be trusted. If we make a treaty with them they will break it, for they are liars. Let there be perpetual war with the Osages.' " [6]

In a burst of exasperation the general concluded his venture in shuttle diplomacy by informing the Cherokee that he was washing his hands of the whole affair. He told them to make peace in their own way, or, failing that, settle the matter to their satisfaction so long as they did not "interfere with the persons or property of white people." [7]

6. Rev. Cephas Washburn, A. M., *Reminiscences of the Indians* (Richmond: Presbyterian Committee of Publication, 1869), p. 114.

In March the *Gazette* carried an account of the spreading tribal war: "Both parties have been eager for bloody combat. . . . As both are powerful nations a long and sanguinary conflict may be expected. The Osage are said to be the strongest in point of numbers, but the Cherokee are much the best supplied with arms and ammunition." [8] Governor Miller viewed the hostilities as a "marauding, thieving cowardly kind of warfare" and from that time forward treated Indian affairs with disdain. The skirmishing in the west, although it would increase in intensity and alarm the white settlers, was not sufficient to keep him at his post, which he vacated for as long as eighteen months at a stretch in order to visit his family in New England. His ambitious stand-in, Territorial Secretary Robert Crittenden, improved upon his absence by taking control of the affairs of government in a fashion that established Arkansas's first patronage-based political machine.

In 1825 the hero of Lundy's Lane withdrew to a more civilized sinecure as collector of customs at the Port of Salem. The record of the Miller administration is too sketchy to permit a judgment as to whether it reflects a humane disposition, at sharp variance with the mores of the brawling frontier community, or a singular indolence. Nuttall provides only a passing glimpse of the general. The botanist was intrigued by what may have been the first criminal case of record to complete the process of adjudication under Arkansas law. This was the trial of Thomas Dickinson for rape inflicted upon the "almost infant person of a daughter of his late wife." Nuttall was shocked by the fashion in which the statutes of Arkansas, adapted from the Missouri code, sought to fit the punishment to the crime: "Castration is no less singular and barbarous, however just, than the heinous nature of the crime itself." [9] Governor Miller may have shared his view. In what must have been one of his earliest official acts he pardoned the convicted rapist.

Crude as it undoubtedly was, Arkansas Post was rising above

---

7. Edwin C. Bearss and A. M. Gibson, *Fort Smith: Little Gibraltar on The Arkansas* (Norman: University of Oklahoma Press, 1969), p. 45.

8. Grant Foreman, *Indians and Pioneers* (Norman: University of Oklahoma Press, 1936), p. 89.

9. Nuttall, *Journey of Travels,* p. 56.

the somnolent simplicities of the frontier trading post it had been throughout its considerable history. There were lawyers now, and land speculators, and politicians, for most of whom the roles were interchangeable. William Woodruff, an ambitious New York printer, had arrived with the storied "shirt-tail full of type" and was producing a remarkably literate journal, the *Arkansas Gazette,* which has survived to become the oldest newspaper west of the Mississippi. The War Department had signified the forward march of the frontier by deploying its forces hundreds of miles to the west. And the capital itself was soon to migrate to a more central location.

3

"To Restore Tranquility"

N 1821 the capital of Arkansas was relocated near the geographic center of the territory, and Arkansas Post slid into obscurity as a minor river port. In general the new site was dictated by the lay of the land. About halfway along its southeasterly course from Fort Smith to the Mississippi the Arkansas River abruptly emerges from the low mountain ridges that flank its valley. At that point early travelers took their bearing from Big Rock, a sizable peak that presents a bare stone face north of the river. On the other bank, two miles downstream, there is a much smaller outcropping that came to be known by extension as Little Rock. Here, as it grew, the capital would straddle the natural dividing line between hill country and flatlands.

But the actual siting of the future state's principal city was not a simple matter of logic and convenience. The decision was political, ostensibly in the province of Governor Miller and the elected general assembly. The jockeying came down to a contest between those who favored Little Rock and those backing Cadron, a settlement some twenty miles upstream.

It was land, not peltry, that now brought outlanders flocking into the territory. The first law of the frontier is that where there is cheap public land there will be land speculators, and where there are land speculators there will be lawyers. So there began a mixture of political and legal maneuvering out of which some legislators were able to reap considerable personal benefit—a precedent that has come down intact to the present.

Except for a few claims based on Spanish grants, and the Indian treaty rights which were in the process of being extinguished, all the land in the territory initially belonged to the United States. Some of those who preceded the federal land office simply picked likely plots and began to clear farm sites. Under an 1814 pre-emption law these were given first right of purchase on tracts they had improved. Otherwise the land was divided into convenient parcels and put up for sale at a modest price. Tracts were available free for veterans of military service, and in 1815 replacement land was made available without charge for victims of the New Madrid earthquakes of 1811 and 1812, which relocated stretches of the Mississippi and submerged much arable land in eastern Arkansas and Missouri. Later, substantial tracts were set aside to finance public improvements and were turned over to state and local governing bodies as they came into being.

These land claims were transferable, thereby providing the basis for a freewheeling real estate market that soon produced a number of substantial fortunes. The lawyers who were on the inside of these transactions had ample opportunity to acquire land of their own, and many did so—becoming the richest and most prominent figures in territorial society. It was here in the land warrant market that the capital city was conceived. One of the founding speculators, William Russell, rode down from Saint Louis in the early 1800s to spend long hours in the saddle looking over the virgin lands. Recognizing that the seat of government was bound to move upriver with the spread of population, he duly noted the natural virtues of the site at the Little Rock, and acquired the pre-emption claims of settlers in the area.

Another Missourian, Moses Austin, was looking past Arkansas; as early as 1814 he began hatching a scheme to colonize the Spanish territory beyond Red River, and in 1819 he sent his son, Stephen, to look for a base on the American side. Stephen Austin, who would see the family dream through to fruition and lend his name to the capital of Texas, became familiar with the possibilities of the area where the old road that angled down from southeast Missouri crossed the Arkansas near the Little Rock. With his brother-in-law and several cousins, he came up with a competing claim based on New Madrid certificates.

Against this kind of competition the Cadron supporters were dealt out, and on October 25, 1820, the legislature settled on Little Rock as the new capital. Initially, the Austin group came out on top, their claim recognized by an agreement to build facilities for the government's use. Russell hung on and went to court, where the Austin interest was represented by the redoubtable Chester Ashley. After much legal maneuvering the judgment came down on Russell's side, and the contest passed into a sort of frontier musical comedy phase, with the Austin faction physically removing the townsite's original buildings from Russell's holding. An eyewitness account was provided by a passing traveler, Gen. Thomas James:

> As we approached Little Rock we beheld a scene of true western
> life and character, that no other country could present. First, we saw
> a large wood and stone building in flames, and then about one
> hundred men, painted, masked, and disguised in almost every
> conceivable manner, engaged in removing the town. These men,
> with ropes and chains, would march off a frame house on wheels
> and logs, place it about three or four hundred yards from its former
> site, and then return and move off another in the same manner.
> They all seemed tolerably drunk.[1]

There had to be a compromise, and there was. Russell and Ashley met in the land office at Batesville, each party deeded half its claim to the other, and Ashley went on to a career in law and politics that left him reputed the wealthiest man in Arkansas at the time of his death in 1848.

The real estate boom was the source of inexorable pressure pushing the indigenous Indians westward. The first victims, the Quapaw, were in no condition to resist. The large and hospitable tribe that welcomed the French explorers had been brought to a sorry pass by the white man's diseases, his vices, and finally his ingratitude. The *Arkansas Archeological Survey* found

1. John Gould Fletcher, *Arkansas* (Chapel Hill: University of North Carolina Press, 1947), p. 74.

the Quapaw population reduced to fifteen hundred by 1750, and it declined steadily thereafter. In his *Journal,* Thomas Nuttall wrote of his first encounter with the native Indians at Arkansas Post: "Their errand was whiskey, and I regretted that it was not possible to satisfy them without it. . . . I was sorry to find that they were beggars, and that one of them proved himself to be a thief." [2]

In their first treaty in 1804 the incoming Americans recognized the Quapaw claim to all the land between the Arkansas and Red rivers; by 1818 the tribal leaders had been euchred into ceding all this vast expanse, except for a tract south of the Arkansas running from Pine Bluff to Little Rock; in return they received $4,000 in goods and an annuity of $1,000. Nuttall, observing that the Quapaw chief, Hakatton, was "very sensible and intelligent, though much too fond of whiskey," turned his scorn on the United States agents who took advantage of him: "Such are the negotiating conquests of the American republic, made almost without the expense of either blood or treasure!" [3]

In 1824 the Quapaw gave up what was left of their shrunken patrimony in return for a payment that amounted to one dollar per hundred thousand acres. They were then transported to the Caddo country on the Red River, where their Indian brothers made them so unwelcome they soon began drifting back to their ancestral lands. Although they were described in a report to the secretary of war as "a kind of inoffensive people [who] aid the Whites in picking out their cotton and furnishing them with game," Washington denied their petition to settle on some "inferior lands" near Pine Bluff. [4] When they were finally relocated on a small reservation in what was to become Indian Territory their number was estimated at less than five hundred.

The Indians north of the Arkansas were a tougher breed. Old Major Lovely, out on the front line between the Cherokee and the Osage, wore himself out sending messages to Washington

---

2. Thomas Nuttall, *Journey of Travels in the Arkansas Territory During the Year 1819* (Philadelphia: Thomas Palmer, 1821), p. 94.

3. Nuttall, *Journey of Travels,* p. 132.

4. Fletcher, *Arkansas,* p. 82.

urging that troops be sent in to head off what was approaching the proportions of a full-scale tribal war. But the major was dead and gone by the time the War Department responded with orders to establish what would become the mother post in the network of army installations that for the next half century was charged with pacifying the new frontier.

In December 1817, at Belle Point, a bluff overlooking the junction of the Arkansas and Poteau rivers, a log stockade was laid out under the command of Maj. William Bradford. His mission was set forth by Gen. Thomas A. Smith, after whom the post was named: ". . . to prevent the Indian tribes in that quarter continuing hostilities with each other, you are required to represent to the Chiefs and warriors of those Tribes the wish of the President on this subject and use every legal means in your power to restore tranquility among them." [5]

Bradford was assigned a company of the Rifle Regiment, a crack unit specially trained in scouting and patrol duty and garbed in its own distinctive gray uniform. The frontier held no unknown terrors for the major. As a captain in the Seventeenth Infantry in the War of 1812 he took a shot in the left thigh at Fort Meigs, Michigan, and his commanding officer, citing him for gallantry, reported that he was back in action "before his wounds had healed sufficiently to enable him to walk without a crutch, hobbling along at the head of his company, upon more than one occasion directing the fire of his musketry against the warriors of Tecumseh." [6]

Bradford was described by a fellow officer as a small, stern-looking man, who brought with him a reputation as a strict disciplinarian, a quality Fort Smith quickly put to the test. For the five years he served there he was chronically short of men and supplies. His company was supposed to muster seventy enlisted men, including three sergeants, four corporals, a drummer, and a fifer; it was rarely up to strength, and much of the time the duty roster was reduced by those who may have been sick, and some

5. Edwin C. Bearss and A. M. Gibson, *Fort Smith: Little Gibraltar on the Arkansas* (Norman: University of Oklahoma Press, 1969), pp. 15, 16.

6. Carolyn Thomas Foreman, "William Bradford," *Arkansas Historical Quarterly* 13 (Winter 1954): 342.

who certainly were drunk. One way or another the lonely soldiers found the means to improve upon the gill of whiskey the army in those days issued with each daily ration.

As the only resident representative of the United States Government in the remote territory, Bradford was the recipient of unrealistic and contradictory orders, and of an undue share of the blame when he attempted to carry them out. In May 1819, the War Department ordered him to clear the Red River country west of the Kiamichi of white Arkansas squatters who had illegally infiltrated Indian treaty lands. It is to be hoped that the major at least enjoyed the scenery along the way, lyrically described by Nuttall, who rode south with him:

> Our route was continued through prairies, occasionally divided by sombre belts of timber, which serve to mark the course of the rivulets. These vast plains, beautiful almost as the fancied Elysium, were now enamelled with innumerable flowers, among the most splendid of which were the azure larkspur . . . fragrant phloxes, and the purple psilotria. Serene and charming as the blissful regions of fancy, nothing here appeared to exist but what contributes to harmony.[7]

Nothing, that is, except the expatriate Arkansans, who greeted with outspoken resentment the War Department's orders to remove themselves from the Indian lands. Nuttall, lowering his gaze from Elysium, found these disaffected wards of Major Bradford to "bear the worst moral character imaginable, being many of them renegadoes from justice, and such as have forefeited the esteem of civilized society." [8] Upon his return from Indian country, the perceptive Nuttall deplored the decision of the federal government to use the territory as a dumping ground for traditionally hostile tribes, thereby creating the "necessity for establishing among them an expensive military agency, and coercing them by terror." [9]

Whether or not Major Bradford's undernourished military command could properly be called expensive, it was busy. The

7. Nuttall, *Journey of Travels,* p. 208.
8. Nuttall, *Journey of Travels,* pp. 221, 222.
9. Nuttall, *Journey of Travels,* p. 122.

skirmishing between the Cherokee and the Osage continued, and at every round produced increased demands from the white settlers for protection. Bradford, in his ordained role as peace-maker, expressed optimism in an early report to Secretary of War Calhoun on March 28, 1818: "I am endeavoring to effect a general meeting between these two tribes in the month of May, to produce if possible a perfect reconciliation." [10] By 1821, after he had, at Calhoun's behest, enlisted the aid of the civilian head of Arkansas Territory, his sights were perceptibly lower. The Cherokee Council, responding to Governor Miller's notice that he was leaving it up to them to obtain satisfaction from their Osage enemies in their own way, wrote to Major Bradford: "We expect to have to go to war with our neighbors in a very short time and there is a good many of you people in our way." [11]

Under the circumstances the major's report to Calhoun on August 10, 1821, is remarkably restrained:

> I have so far succeeded with the Cherokees and Osages as to raise doubts in their minds of the propriety of their going to War contrary to the known will of the Government. . . . I felt some delicacy in interfering while Gov. Miller was here, inasmuch as his and my views on Indian subjects differ. I found it folly to appeal to their understanding. The only way I have found to manage them is by appeal to their fears. [12]

Bradford also had his problems on the political front. Only the Fort Smith commandant and the territorial governor were authorized to issue licenses for trading on Indian treaty lands. During one of Miller's prolonged absences, Crittenden, as acting governor, handed out more than two hundred permits to his followers authorizing them to hunt, trap, and trade with the Indians west of Fort Smith. When the War Department upheld Bradford's refusal to recognize these licenses it became his duty to hunt down and evict Crittenden's cronies.

10. Territorial Papers of the United States, Volume 19, Arkansas Territory, 1819–1825, p. 58.

11. Grant Foreman, *Indians and Pioneers* (Norman: University of Oklahoma Press, 1969), p. 45.

12. Territorial Papers, Vol. 19, p. 64.

On February 16, 1822, an entire regiment, the Seventh Infantry under Col. Matthew Arbuckle, arrived at Fort Smith to assume the duties carried out by the little major's hard-bitten handful. Bradford mounted his last parade on the bluffs above the river and saw the only surviving company of the storied Rifle Regiment disappear into the ranks of the Seventh. He had done his duty, but at the expense of becoming persona non grata with the Osage, the Cherokee, the white squatters, and the political leaders at Little Rock. "Bradford had, through his tenacity and high sense of responsibility, created a nucleus for law, order, and the vanguard of a community and ultimate civilization," the Fort Smith historians, Edwin C. Bearrs and A. M. Gibson, wrote. "He had protected the interest and integrity of the United States on its farthest frontier." [13]

Bradford was reassigned to Fort Selden at Natchitoches, Louisiana, where he reported to a future president, Lt. Col. Zachary Taylor. There, on April 20, 1822, the little major resigned his commission, in the process levying a claim for money due from the government in which he offered his own laconic summary of his career as a regular officer:

> I have claims on the government of suspended vouchers for the year 1812. If it is said why not attended to before I answer that I have been so sent about from the North Western Army to the Creek War, and to the Red River from thence to the Upper Mississippi and thence here, that the Government has given me no time to attend to them. They kept me as busy as a nailer. [14]

The adjutant general refused to authorize the trip to Washington, and it is not clear how Bradford's claim was settled. He turned up as civilian sutler at Fort Towson, one of the new posts established under Colonel Arbuckle's command, and in 1823 he stood for territorial delegate from Arkansas, to be defeated by Henry W. Conway. On April 14, 1825, he was awarded a monthly pension of $15 in compensation for the old wound inflicted by Tecumseh's braves, and he received belated recognition from the territorial government by appointment as briga-

13. Bearrs and Gibson, *Fort Smith,* pp. 53, 54.
14. Territorial Papers, Vol. 19, p. 309.

dier general of Arkansas militia. On October 20, 1826, the little major died of yellow fever. He was fifty-five years old. They buried him at Fort Smith, where he surely deserves a special place of honor in what is now the United States National Cemetery.

4

Civilization on the March

 Y the time Arkansas achieved territorial status the full weight of the federal government was shifting toward the effort to "extinguish" the old treaty guarantees and clear the resident tribes from the southeastern states. The first major treaty negotiated in the thrust for Indian removal was signed on October 18, 1820, with the Choctaw yielding rights to their hereditary lands in Mississippi in exchange for a new domain lying between the Arkansas and Red rivers. This would have handed over to the Choctaw two of the new territory's seven counties and parts of two others, an area already occupied by 5,000 white settlers. The treaty produced such consternation in Arkansas that even the sainted Andrew Jackson, who had signed as one of the federal commissioners, was not immune to criticism.

However, by May 12, 1821, the *Gazette* could report that the territorial delegate to Congress, James Woodson Bates, had presented to President Monroe a remonstrance "against the odious terms of the treaty with the Choctaw and he assured them that another treaty would be negotiated to rectify the one of October last." [1] The matter remained in dispute until 1825, when the Choctaw, under pressure, agreed to accept a line running due

---

1. Grant Foreman, *Indians and Pioneers* (Norman: University of Oklahoma Press, 1936), p. 149.

south from Fort Smith to the Red River as the eastern boundary of their treaty lands.

Treaties negotiated in 1818 and 1825 extinguished the Osage title to the area covered by the present Benton and Washington counties in the northwest corner of the state; the Quapaw signed away the last of their birthright in 1824; in 1823 the Cherokee lands were confined to an area north of the Arkansas River, and by 1828 the boundary had been pushed west to a line running north from Fort Smith. This process freed the present state's territory of tribal reservations, and on May 28, 1830, the Congress recognized the limits thus established as the boundary between Arkansas and the new Indian Territory created on that day.

Arkansas, however, was not yet done with Indian affairs. While the garrison at Fort Smith was relocated in new posts farther west, the army's administrative headquarters remained at the Arkansas site for most of the period up to the Civil War. And the new border was porous to both Indians and whites, so that clashes continued for many years. Then, from 1830 to 1839, Arkansans were witnesses to, and sometimes participants in, one of the great tragic dramas in the nation's history—the removal of the Five Civilized Tribes from east of the Mississippi to the new Indian Territory. Under military escort, sometimes in chains, scores of thousands of Cherokee, Seminole, Choctaw, Creek, and Chickasaw passed across Arkansas on foot and by boat, following what the Cherokee, with good reason, called the Trail of Tears.

The tribes involved in the diaspora ordained by the Indian Removal Act that became law on May 28, 1830, were designated as civilized under standards applied by those who were now forcing them into exile. On the eastern seaboard, in the Carolinas, Georgia, and Florida, the Indians had been in contact with white settlers for two hundred years. Many had white blood, dressed in conventional garb, and professed Christianity. They had developed agriculture along the lines of the plantation system growing up around them, and it followed that a substantial number were slaveholders. In their previous domains they had established their own codes of law, police, and courts, and had welcomed missionaries who came among them as educators.

The great Cherokee, Sequoyah, who lived for some years in Arkansas, had devised an Indian alphabet, and the communications of the tribal elders were usually literate and often eloquent.

The fact that they had thus begun to adapt to the superimposed culture of the whites lent special poignancy to the treatment they now received. If they had remained seminomads, accustomed to living off the land, a trek of a thousand miles or more to a new hunting ground might have been no great hardship. But for the most part these were then people with goods and chattels, used to settled indoor living, no longer capable of organizing themselves under the ancient tribal division of labor. Reference to the Great White Father in Washington recurs over and over in the treaties, and in the communications in which the Indians protest their violation, and the term had quite literal meaning for them—for at this stage of their acculturation their leaders recognized the need for a paternal government to protect them against the depredations of the whites, and against their own weaknesses.

The duplicity and bad faith of the agents of the Great White Father were matched by their incompetence. The army organized the overland expeditions and provided escort, but private contractors were commissioned to supply the emigrants en route. This arrangement produced a saturnalia of fraud, in which a good many Arkansans cheerfully took part.

Contemporary accounts provide a grim record of the forced migration. In the closing months of 1836 nearly fourteen thousand Creek were strung out in an almost continuous line between Little Rock and Fort Gibson in Indian Territory. A letter in the *New York Observer* dated December 25 described the scene at Little Rock on that Christmas Day:

> They consist of all ages, sexes, and sizes, and all of the varieties of human intellect and condition, from the civilized and tenderly nourished matron and misses, to the wild savage, and the poorest of the poor. Thousands of them are entirely destitute of shoes or cover of any kind for their feet; many of them are almost naked. . . . they are wading in cold mud, or are hurried on over the frozen ground as the case may be. Many of them have had in this way their

feet frost-bitten, and . . . are left on the road to await the ability or convenience of the contractors to assist them. Many of them . . . die, and are thrown by the side of the road, and are covered over only with brush, etc.—where they remain until devoured by the wolves.[2]

The Creek were traveling under a ''negotiated'' agreement but they were, if anything, worse off than those Indians who had resisted removal until rounded up by the army. Among the last contingents to pass Little Rock was a party of Seminoles who held out in the swamps of Florida until a military expedition brought them out as captives. There were 453 of these, about one-third black, aboard the steamboat *Renown* out of New Orleans. The *Gazette* reported:

Among those who have gone up are about 150 Spanish Indians or Spaniards who have intermarried with the Seminoles. Take the whole party as a body, it is the most dirty, naked, and squalid one that we have seen. Armed sentries and U.S. soldiers were stationed in different parts of the boat, and not one Indian was permitted to step ashore during the few hours the boat laid at our landing.[3]

If there are any heroes in this sordid saga they are to be found among the junior officers of the army and the Marine Corps who were assigned to escort duty. Their reports to the War Department record their outrage at the conduct of the civilian suppliers and local fixers, over whom the officers had no real authority. They did not hesitate to make known their view of the basic injustice of the undertaking. And they went far beyond the call of duty in trying to ease the suffering of their charges. Some very strong men confessed that they wept when they gazed upon the women and children who marched in the lines they policed.

The primary source of their frustration was the great void between white and Indian culture that still existed beneath the veneer of "civilization." Lt. Isaac P. Simonton, describing the ordeal of bringing a party of Choctaw overland from the White River to Little Rock, wrote:

Nothing can exceed the tardiness with which an Indian performs anything like manual labor. He forms no estimate of the value of

2. Foreman, *Indian Removal*, p. 177.
3. Foreman, *Indian Removal*, p. 365.

time. . . . He labors therefore only when necessity compels him. . . . So perfectly inefficient are they, that on one occasion my assistant, Mr. Montgomery, and myself were obliged to get off our horses and put a man into a cart, who was in the last stages of Cholera, although there were more than fifty of his own people standing by. This was not the effect of want of humanity, but a sheer want of energy. Having received assistance once, they would not bury their own dead afterward without asking for help.[4]

A civilian hero turns up in the account of Lt. J. W. Harris, whose expedition was grounded at Cadron Creek in May 1834. While his contingent of some two hundred Cherokee was camped there cholera broke out. The young officer located a country doctor, Jesse C. Roberts, a few miles away, and he came in the night to begin his ministrations. For some days Dr. Roberts tended his Cherokee patients around the clock, bringing in his family to help. When at last the disease seemed under control the doctor collapsed, and Lieutenant Harris recorded his demise:

I have devoted the day to my poor friend. He has none to help him. His poor weakly wife can scarcely crawl about; the only servant is better out of the way, or has her hands full to keep this houseful of children from their dying father. The two or three miserable white people who are scattered within so many miles of his cabin, though sent for, will not come. They are panic struck.[5]

Those who ministered to the soul of the red man hardly had an easier time. Roman Catholic priests brought the cross along with the sword of the Spanish and French explorers, and the Protestant denominations had missions among the eastern tribes well before the Revolution. The first of these to be established in Arkansas was the handiwork of a hardy Yankee Congregationalist, Cephas Washburn, who, after being ordained in his native Vermont, went down to spread the gospel among the Georgia Cherokee. At that time the tribe was beginning to congregate in Arkansas, and in 1819 the American Board of Foreign Missions in New York proposed sending teachers among them. The Reverend Mr. Washburn and three others got the call.

4. Foreman, *Indian Removal*, p. 94.

5. Foreman, *Indian Removal*, p. 259.

In his *Reminiscences of the Indians* Washburn lays claim to preaching the first sermon ever delivered at Little Rock. When his little party, plagued by illness in the course of the arduous journey by keelboat up the Arkansas, stopped to buy medicine, he was importuned by Col. Stephen Austin to deliver a Fourth of July sermon. He did so, but gives no clue as to his text, only noting that he addressed the faithful in "a small log cabin made of round logs, with the bark on . . . to an audience of fourteen men and no women." [6]

Washburn and his company proceeded upriver and in 1820 established their mission near the present Russellville, naming it after Pres. Timothy Dwight of Yale. The missionaries and their wives set about building dwellings for themselves, a meeting house, and a school. The relationship with the Cherokee was amiable, and in time Washburn would be received as a brother by the leading men of the tribe.

Within two years Washburn's school, probably the first of any kind to be established in Arkansas Territory, had an enrollment of some eighty Cherokee boys and girls. In 1828 Dwight Mission housed eight missionary families, all from New England, and the compound encompassed thirty buildings. This was largely a subsistence operation, since the contribution of the mission board ran to about a thousand dollars a year in cash and a few boxes of groceries and clothing.

With all of this hard manual labor to be done, wrestling with the devil never lost priority. The Reverend H. R. Wilson, who joined Washburn in 1832, recalled his arrival at the mission on Christmas morning. He was sent to the home of Colonel Webber, a Cherokee chief who did not accept Christ as his Savior, but who agreed that it would be better if his braves spent the holy day with the missionaries "instead of drinking whiskey and dancing, as had been their custom for many years. . . . During the day we had not less than six to eight sermons, to all of which the Indians listened attentively, though often shivering with cold." It is perhaps not irreverent to wonder how many in that congregation agreed with the Reverend Mr. Wilson, who

6. Rev. Cephas Washburn, A. M., *Reminiscences of the Indians* (Richmond: Presbyterian Committee of Publication, 1869), pp. 96, 97.

recorded this as "the happiest Christmas I had ever spent." [7]

The outward marks of civilization did appear under their ministry. Washburn reported to the board: "There has been a great change since we came among them. At that time there were not twenty men in the nation who wore hats and pantaloons. Now there are not twenty who do not wear pantaloons, and the great majority wear hats. The majority of the females now wear bonnets, many of them Leghorn." [8]

Dwight Mission moved west sixty miles to Indian Territory when the Cherokee were relocated across the border, and continued to thrive until the Civil War. Washburn retired in 1840 and answered the call of the Arkansas Presbytery to preach the Calvinist doctrine in the growing towns of the state. His brethren in the missions continued to match their faith with works, although many were to be rewarded by tribal excommunication when their abolitionist sympathies began to alarm the powerful slaveholding Indian families who were to make Indian Territory a Confederate province.

Looking back across a century and half from the vantage point of a skeptical age one may wonder whether these selfless men and women came any closer to bridging the cultural gap than did the soldiers who often found it necessary to do battle with the Indians even as they tried to protect them against the ravages of the civilization they brought to the frontier. Some, at least, of the military men had second thoughts about their mission, but there is no hint of self-doubt in Cephas Washburn's summation of his life and times:

> Our Indians were contemplated as a part of the fallen descendants of Adam. . . . True, there was commiseration for their savage state, and a desire to elevate them by intellectual culture and the introduction among them of the arts and uses of civilized life; but the paramount pity for them was that they were sinners and in danger of eternal perdition, and the paramount aim and effort was to make known to them the only way to be saved from sin and eternal woe. . . . We labored long and prayed often, and with strong crying and tears. [9]

7. Washburn, *Reminiscences*, pp. 44, 45.
8. Washburn, *Reminiscences*, pp. 23, 24.
9. Washburn, *Reminiscences*, p. 123.

5

"Heated in That Political Furnace"

*T*HE kind of self-generating violence that is the hallmark of the frontier continued in Arkansas long after the leading edge of the westward migration had passed. Conflicts of interest deemed to be colored by questions of personal honor required that the offended party obtain satisfaction on his own motion. For ordinary frontiersmen this meant resort to whatever weapon was handy; for those who considered themselves gentlemen it meant the *code duello*.

The protocol for the dawn meeting under the oaks had been imported to the United States in colonial days, and adapted to republican forms. At least one duelist of note, Andrew Jackson, made it to the White House, and another, Aaron Burr, might have done so had he not shot down Alexander Hamilton en route. It was not until 1838 that Congress outlawed dueling in the District of Columbia. The sole vote cast against the measure in the upper house was that of Sen. Ambrose H. Sevier of Arkansas, who argued the case on practical grounds. "The upshot of the bill will be to make each of us require a corporal's guard to attend us from our lodgings to the Senate, because men will not be able to give satisfaction to those we abuse," he said, predicting that the traffic would be so heavy the standing army would have to be increased by half.[1]

Sevier's irony certainly was applicable in his home state,

---

1. Margaret Ross, "Chronicles of Arkansas," *Arkansas Gazette,* July 9, 1967.

where the political process was never effectively insulated from physical violence until well after the Civil War. In 1819 a member of the territory's initial house of representatives, William O. Allen, called out Robert C. Oden, a disciple of Arkansas's first political boss, Secretary Robert Crittenden. This affair, apparently triggered by a trivial personal difference, culminated in the death of Allen as the duelists, accompanied by seconds, surgeons, and a fair number of spectators, repaired to a sand bar in the river below Arkansas Post. More meticulous men soon established the custom of honoring the antidueling laws by removing themselves from territorial, and later state, jurisdiction. When two judges of the superior court met in mortal combat in 1824 the site was on the east bank of the Mississippi opposite the mouth of the Arkansas. Other favored spots were on the Louisiana or Texas side of Red River, and, after the organization of Indian Territory, across the Arkansas from Fort Smith.

In the case of the judicial duelists there was a delay of six weeks after the challenge was issued so that the principals could wind up cases pending at the current term of court. They met with pistols at ten paces and Judge Andrew Scott's first shot brought down Judge Joseph Selden with a mortal wound. On the eve of the duel Scott wrote to his wife what would have been a farewell note had the exchange gone the other way: "I hope you will be satisfied that I am not tired of living, but merely that I prefer taking the *chance* of, or even death itself, to life in *disgrace*." [2]

Since the judges were presidential appointees, the Arkansas authorities held that they had no power to invoke the provision that public officials guilty of dueling should be removed from public office. William Woodruff, who at the beginning of his career declared against the *code duello* on principle, referred in the *Gazette* to "the long-talked of and much-ridiculed duel." And over in Tennessee the *Nashville Whig* noted that "two of the Judges of the highest court in the Territory recently determined a difference on the bench by an appeal to arms. . . .

2. Ross, "Chronicles of Arkansas," *Arkansas Gazette*, Sept. 12, 1965.

Quere: If such is the judiciary, what sort of folks are the common people?" [3]

The common people were precisely the same sort, if somewhat more impromptu, and even had a fairly well settled code of their own. Charles E. Nash in his *Pioneers of Arkansas* provides an eyewitness account of what apparently was a fairly routine encounter on the streets of the capital. During the legislative session of 1836 Maj. Archibald Greer, secretary of the senate, was en route to Peay's Hotel when "a large, stout muscular man struck the major on the head with his fist, and at the same time tripped him so that he fell on his back. The man then mounted him and placing his thumbs in his eyes, was about starting them from their sockets, when the major cried out, 'Pretty good idea,' slapping both of his fingers in the fellow's eyes made him cry out 'nuff.' Whatever advantage had been gained by fighters in those days, when one cried 'nuff' you must stop, and like the old Roman, desist from further injury." [4]

In the canvass of 1827 Henry W. Conway was re-elected to Congress, defeating Crittenden's candidate, Oden. In the aftermath Conway made public a letter Crittenden construed as calling him a liar, and the territorial secretary promptly challenged. While that duel was pending Conway's cousin, Ambrose Sevier, went off to exchange shots with Thomas W. Newton, a Crittenden supporter, without fatal result. Crittenden and Conway met at dawn on the east bank of the Mississippi, and the delegate was fatally wounded in the first exchange.

Chester Ashley, then emerging as the mastermind behind the Conway faction, was called out in turn by Oden and Crittenden's brother, Thomas, but took advantage of a provision of the *code duello* that permitted a married man to decline on the ground that his challengers were bachelors without comparable family responsibilities. There were numerous unpremeditated but no less sanguinary encounters among the political antagonists. Judge Scott, who weighed only 130 pounds, used his

3. Ross, "Chronicles of Arkansas," *Arkansas Gazette,* Sept. 12, 1965.
4. Ross, "Chronicles of Arkansas," *Arkansas Gazette,* Dec. 3, 1958.

sword cane to dispatch Edmund Hogan, an assailant twice his size; when William Montgomery, a friend of Conway, met Thomas Wyatt Johnston, an associate of Crittenden, the pair exchanged pistol shots across the street, then fell back on canes and dirks.

In the special election for Congress to replace his slain kinsman, Sevier handily defeated two opponents, one of whom was the durable Judge Scott. In the course of that bloodshot campaign the territory's only newspaper proprietor abandoned the last pretense of journalistic neutrality. As the political leaders began to choose up sides, splitting law partnerships and other business arrangements, William Woodruff perfected what was to be a long-standing and highly profitable alliance with Ashley, Sevier, and assorted relatives of the late Henry W. Conway.

This organization formed around a group of immigrants from Tennessee who arrived well versed in the workings of the spoils system. Several branches of a prominent family with close political ties to Andrew Jackson united on the frontier, where the leading members held commissions as federally appointed land surveyors. Inside track to the best land was bestowed by William Rector, the surveyor general in Saint Louis, on four of his brothers and four nephews, three of whom were sons of his sister, Ann Conway. Another relative, Ambrose H. Sevier, married the daughter of Benjamin Johnson, brother of Richard H. Johnson, the pro-Jackson Kentuckian who served as vice-president under Martin Van Buren.

In antebellum Arkansas kinsmen bearing the names Rector, Conway, Sevier, and Johnson provided two territorial delegates, two United States senators, and three governors. This "Dynasty," as it came to be called, controlled the Democratic party. The Arkansas historian, George H. Thompson, noted: "It is ironic that Andrew Jackson's rise to political power, though popularly identified with the common man, was the basis for establishing an aristocratic dominance of Arkansas politics." [5]

Crittenden, whose political lineage went back to Kentucky

5. George H. Thompson, *Arkansas and Reconstruction* (Port Washington, N.Y.: Kennikat Press, 1976), p. 20.

and another of Jackson's mortal enemies, Henry Clay, had consolidated his position in the years when he virtually ran the territorial government during the intermittent administration of Governor Miller. But in 1825 the Dynasty acquired a potent ally in the person of Arkansas's second governor, Maj. Gen. George Izard, the strong-minded scion of an old Charleston Huguenot family, who immediately trimmed Crittenden's authority to the strict limits of the secretary's office. The new alignment was evident in the appointment of Ashley, Conway, and Sevier as gubernatorial aides with the militia rank of lieutenant colonel, while Ashley also positioned himself on the inside as Izard's legal advisor.

All of these leading figures were engaged in land speculation, and their interests often conflicted. These considerations, accentuated by hypersensitive personal pride, coincided with related matters of direct political patronage, including the public printing upon which newspapers everywhere then depended. This guaranteed that the *Gazette* would not long stand alone; the *Arkansas Advocate* entered the field in 1830 as a Crittenden organ, and other rival publications followed as the political factions shifted and regrouped.

"Mr. Woodruff, my employer, being an honest and sober man, the majority of the people are his bitter enemies, and he has frequently been threatened," Hiram Whittington, the *Gazette's* Yankee composing room foreman, wrote to his brother in the course of the 1827 campaign.[6] When the newspaper published an anonymous letter implying the misuse of territorial funds, Crittenden demanded the name of the author so that retribution could be administered by "cowhiding, dirking, earcropping and shooting." Woodruff made his reply in the columns of the *Gazette,* offering Crittenden space for rebuttal, and in effect reasserting his policy against dueling: "I conceive it to be the duty of all editors . . . to assume the responsibility of such communications themselves. . . . I now announce that I am prepared to sustain these charges, if you think proper to

6. Margaret Ross, *Arkansas Gazette: The Early Years 1819–66* (Little Rock: Arkansas Gazette Foundation, 1969), p. 71.

require me to do so, in a legal manner." [7] Surprisingly, Crittenden responded with a libel suit, later settled out of court. But
this did nothing to take the heat out of the raging political controversy.

A few weeks later Whittington wrote to his brother:

> Night before last I saw four pistols presented to as many hearts.
> . . . That there will be bloodshed before the election is over, there
> is not much doubt. Mr. Crittenden, Secretary of the Territory, has
> threatened to cut Mr. Woodruff's throat for publishing a
> communication concerning his official conduct, and, what is much
> worse, has threatened to cut off the nose of every printer in the
> place and pull down the printing office. [8]

Violence did enter upon the premises of the *Gazette* when a
deputy sheriff in Crittenden's camp, John T. Garrett, confronted
Chester Ashley, who was visiting Woodruff. In the confusion
Garrett fired twice and Ashley once; Woodruff wound up with a
flesh wound in his arm, and Garrett took a round in the ab-
domen that brought him death a few hours later. Woodruff and
Ashley were cleared, although conflicting accounts of the affray
would crop up in the course of political and newspaper controversy for years to come. Crittenden was charged in connection with the death of Conway, but, as was the custom in the
case of dueling, he was promptly freed.

The new party designations being perfected in the course of
national political realignment were beginning to take on meaning in the territory. In its very first issue the *Gazette* had nailed
to its masthead the partisan banner Andrew Jackson changed
from National Republican to Democratic, and in time the Crittenden faction came to be identified as Whig. In November,
1828, before the returns for Jackson's landslide victory were in,
Governor Izard died at Little Rock, and Crittenden used his connections with Secretary of State Henry Clay to seek appointment
as his successor. Sevier, however, announced his "unconquer-
able hatred" for the territorial secretary, and the matter was
passed over pending Jackson's inauguration. Shortly thereafter

7. Ross, *Arkansas Gazette,* p. 75.
8. Ross, *Arkansas Gazette,* p. 79.

the old spoilsman appointed John Pope, an anti-Clay Kentuckian. A month later Crittenden's head rolled with the announcement that the new territorial secretary would be William Savin Fulton of Alabama, who had once served as Jackson's military secretary, and ultimately would succeed Pope as Arkansas's last appointed governor.

Crittenden was out of office, but not out of politics. His *Arkansas Advocate* recognized the reality of political patronage by declaring its support for Jackson, and through the medium of an anonymous letter expressed surprise that such staunch Jacksonians as Pope and Fulton would continue to bestow favors on Woodruff, who had voted for John Quincy Adams in the recent election. Woodruff admitted his defection but declared a change of heart, and the *Gazette* retained a major share of public printing. The Crittenden connection with the *Advocate* was soon evident, and by the next election the newspaper's Whig identification was explicit. "Political contests were carried on with much acrimony and violence, and abuse filled both the papers," Albert Pike wrote of his tenure on the *Advocate:* "Arkansas bore but a poor character abroad, and I dare not say she did not deserve it." [9]

At sixty, and with only one arm, Governor Pope was pretty well immune to the *code duello,* but he imported from Kentucky as his aide a nephew, Maj. William Fontaine Pope, who was soon under the oaks on the Mississippi shore exchanging shots with a family friend—an affair that came to a head as a result of anonymous letters published in the *Gazette*. A year later young Pope died of wounds suffered in a duel fought on the Texas side of Red River with the journalist-politician Charles Fenton Mercer Noland, the quarrel arising out of letters published in the *Advocate* and the *Gazette*.

As the years went by and the newspapers multiplied the editors began to seek more than verbal satisfaction from each other. In 1840 Edward Cole of the *Gazette* publicly horsewhipped David Lambert of the *Star*. In 1844, Benjamin J. Borden of the *Gazette* wound up on the field of honor facing

9. Ross, "Chronicles of Arkansas," *Arkansas Gazette,* Sept. 15, 1958.

Solon Borland, editor of the *Arkansas Banner*. The editors met on the dueling ground opposite Fort Smith, and Borden, seriously wounded, survived largely because of the ministrations of Borland, a physician, who sprang forward to attend his antagonist once he had shot him down. The two subsequently professed undying friendship, but the capital's fulminating newspaper feud continued, setting the partisan pace for the journals now emerging in all the principal towns. In 1844 the *Gazette,* with no indication of disapprobation, noted an encounter on the field of honor between John D. Logan of the *Van Buren Western Frontier Whig* and George W. Clarke of the *Van Buren Intelligencer.*

   Crittenden, defending himself against charges that his actions had permeated territorial politics with violence, transferred the blame to the *Gazette:* "All the blood that has flowed in Arkansas, from political altercations, has been heated in that political furnace." [10] This may be discounted as self-serving, but the fact remains that the newspapers not only incited bloodshed by their editorial comments and the publication of correspondence attacking public figures, but sold "card" advertisements calculated to invoke formal challenges to combat. In 1848, when Woodruff and Ashley broke with the Dynasty to back Solon Borland in a successful race against their former cohort, Senator Sevier, Borland was challenged by a Sevier supporter. Borland replied that only Sevier had the right to demand satisfaction, and stood on his refusal to meet his challenger even when subjected to the classic personal insult in a card published in the *Banner* declaring him "a liar, a poltroon, and a coward, and unworthy of the notice of any honorable men." [11] Shortly thereafter, George B. Hayden, editor of the *Gazette,* was similarly branded by a card in the *Banner* and replied: "We don't fight duels under any circumstances. They are out of fashion. . . ." [12]

   This judgment may have been premature, but it did signify that public men had begun to recognize that they could refuse to

10. Ross, *Arkansas Gazette,* p. 102.
11. Ross, *Arkansas Gazette,* p. 256.
12. Ross, *Arkansas Gazette,* p. 264.

defend their honor under the code without a politically disastrous loss of face. By 1858 the *True Democrat* was beginning to refer to the *code duello* in the past tense:

> No man could be a political leader, either in the parties of the state or in those of the counties, unless he stood ready at all times to defend his principles at the point of a bowie knife or the muzzle of a pistol. . . . To enumerate all the duels fought between opposing chiefs of the different factions during that sanguinary age would stagger belief. . . . Arkansas has never to this day had a Senator or Representative in the councils of the nation who has not once, if no more, periled his life on the so-called 'field of honor.' [13]

Crittenden did not live to see statehood. Albert Pike, brought to Little Rock as an editor of the *Advocate,* had become a leader of the Whig party, along with the canny lawyer Absalom Fowler. A break between the Dynasty and Governor Pope brought forth a new factional newspaper, the *Times,* which began its career by deploring the condition described by one of its correspondents: "Arkansas has long been ruled by a press [the *Gazette*] and the man who dictates its course [Ashley], with Sevier to act under their direction." [14] In the 1840s Woodruff, occupied by his prospering land business and irritated by what he considered the ingratitude of his political colleagues, pulled out of the contest for a time, selling the *Gazette* to an owner who converted it to the Whig cause. In 1846 the old printer reentered the lists, and in 1850 he bought back his original creation to combine it with his new *Arkansas Democrat,* announcing that he was taking over everything but "the *Gazette's* [Whig] political principles."

These factional and partisan realignments increasingly were affected by national issues. Although they never won a statewide election, the Whigs were strong in the northwestern section of the state, and often carried Little Rock and Pulaski County. In 1840, thousands turned out in the capital at a rally for William Henry Harrison, and it was not only the free cider that caused the cheering for "Tippecanoe and Tyler Too." In

13. Diana Sherwood, "The Code Duello in Arkansas," *Arkansas Historical Quarterly* 6 (Summer 1947): 195.

14. Ross, *Arkansas Gazette,* p. 130.

1842 the state senate divided fourteen Democrats to seven Whigs, and the house forty-two to fourteen.

The special interest of the plantation belt in slavery produced a related obsession with states' rights, providing an unshakable ideological base for the Democratic majority, but the upland farmers and the influential commercial interests in the towns were strongly attracted by Henry Clay's nationalistic program with its emphasis on internal improvements and banking policies intended to promote capitalist expansion. The Arkansas Whigs, like their compatriots elsewhere in the South, had no disposition to confront the Democrats head-on on the issue of slavery, but they sought to change the emphasis under the national leadership of Clay, the Great Compromiser, and for a time they did succeed in dampening the talk of nullification, and later secession, that began to spread through the Deep South.

Arkansans were diverted, too, by external developments to their south and west. Legend has it that the maneuvers that brought Texas independence were plotted at the tavern at Washington in Hempstead County. At least it is certain that Sam Houston, Davy Crockett, and Stephen Austin passed that way, and somewhere in the vicinity Jim Bowie had made for him a long-bladed knife some local historians insist was adapted from the "Arkansas toothpick."

On November 12, 1835, Davy Crockett and six or eight of the Tennesseans who would follow him to the Alamo were in Little Rock, where they were treated to an impromptu banquet by the town's leading citizens. The *Gazette* took respectful note of "the real critter himself," and his mission to free Texas from "the shackles of the Mexican government." Urged by his hosts to tarry and try his famed rifle Betsy on some of the local bear, the frontier hero regretted that his patriotic compulsion would not permit it: "If I could rest anywhere it would be in Arkansaw, where the men are of the real half-horse, half-alligator breed such as grow nowhere else on the face of the universal earth but just around the backbone of North America." [15]

15. Works Progress Administration, *Arkansas: A Guide to the State* (New York: Hastings House, 1941), p. 173.

In 1846 the Mexican War directly involved Arkansas. Troops were raised to replace the regulars transferred to the front from Indian Territory, and a regiment was dispatched to Mexico under Archibald Yell, who resigned his seat in Congress to take command. While many of the Arkansans fought bravely the unit record was less than glorious. The standard history used as a text in the public schools says of the only major engagement of the First Arkansas Cavalry, at Buena Vista: "The Arkansas troops were undisciplined, poorly trained, and overconfident. Though the Americans won the battle, the Arkansas men were routed by Mexican lancers and Colonel Yell was killed. Some of the Arkansas troops who fought in the Mexican War were little better than frontier outlaws." [16]

Quarreling over responsibility for this debacle produced a mutual public caning between two Little Rock editors, and a duel between Albert Pike, a company commander, and John Selden Roane, the regimental executive officer. This affair was described by Margaret Ross in her history of the *Arkansas Gazette:* "After two ineffectual shots were exchanged, the surgeons intervened and the seconds and friends arranged a settlement based on an agreement that there would be no further discussion of the cause of the duel. The state's newspapers heartily agreed, and there the matter ended." [17]

The settlement with Mexico, negotiated by a commission that included Ambrose Sevier, who resigned his U.S. Senate seat to accept the appointment, accelerated the westward movement through Arkansas. In 1849 came the California Gold Rush, and the fields around Van Buren and Fort Smith were white with covered wagons as parties assembled to follow the southern trail through Santa Fe and Fort Yuma. In 1857 a party setting forth from Carroll County in the Ozarks headed north through Utah, and lost seventy-nine men, women, and children in a massacre by Indians and Mormons at Mountain Meadows. Still, the push went on, and the 1860 census showed eleven thousand native Arkansans in Texas and two thousand in California.

16. John L. Ferguson and J. H. Atkinson, *Historic Arkansas* (Little Rock: Arkansas History Commission, 1966), p. 80.

17. Ross, *Arkansas Gazette,* p. 238.

The advance of the frontier drained off some of Arkansas's more spectacular citizens. In May 1851, William Quesenbury wrote back from Sacramento to a friend in Van Buren: "This is very strange country, but it much resembles in its moral aspect our own state about '39 or '40. Gambling, horse racing, and villainy of all kinds . . . several of the gamblers whom you have seen in Arkansas are flourishing in this city." [18]

But there were also migrants Arkansas could ill afford to lose. One of these was George Washington Baines. He first moved to Georgia from his native North Carolina, then settled on a farm near Tuscaloosa long enough to work his way through the University of Alabama. In 1837, he came on to homestead 160 acres on Crooked Creek in Carroll County. Like his father and grandfather before him, Baines was an ordained Baptist minister, and he founded three churches in the Ozarks where he baptized 150 born-again Christians. Elected to the Arkansas legislature in 1842, he served with distinction, displaying a special interest in the common schools. But in 1844 his foot again began to itch, and he moved on to Louisiana. In 1850 he settled finally in Texas, where he left behind a family that included a great-grandson named Lyndon Baines Johnson.

18. Ross, "Chronicles of Arkansas," *Arkansas Gazette*, Nov. 28, 1960.

6

The Peculiar Institution

LAVERY had become a prime national issue by the time Arkansas was recognized as a territory; as statehood approached it became a national obsession. The Missouri Compromise of 1820 was based on the understanding that Missouri would be admitted to the Union as a slave state in return for recognition of the line 36°30′—Arkansas's northern boundary—as the demarcation between free and slave territory in the coming settlement of the West. In the maneuvering that preceded the compromise the House in 1819 rejected by only a two-vote margin an amendment that would have banned the importation of slaves into Arkansas Territory and required the ultimate emancipation of those already there.

The debate was couched almost exclusively in terms of sectional self-interest. The antislavery faction met the states' rights issue by arguing that it did not apply in the case of a territory. Nonslaveholders, they insisted, should have the right to emigrate to Arkansas and try their hand at cultivating cotton and tobacco without having to compete with slave labor. They predicted that opening the West to slavery would make the ban on the African slave trade unenforceable, resulting in the degradation of free white labor everywhere in the nation.

The proponents of slavery conceded the inferior condition of slaves, but argued that their lot would be improved if they were spread over a wider area. And in their turn they contended that southerners would practically be barred from the new territory unless they were allowed to use their black hands for the labor required to open the frontier. None of the southern congressmen defended slavery in its own right, simply standing on the contention that it was an established institution with which northerners should not meddle.

With the support of representatives from the Old Northwest states of Ohio, Indiana, and Illinois the southerners prevailed, and no restrictions were placed on the incoming settlers. There had been blacks in Arkansas since John Law promoted the first effort at mass immigration. John B. Treat, the United States factor assigned to Arkansas Post in 1805, reported that among the sixty or seventy families in the area there were seventy blacks, all slaves except one or two, with seldom more than three to a family. "The pursuits of these people are either Farming, Trading or Hunting . . . but I must admit that agriculture here is still in its infancy." [1] Although the French *Code Noir* was in effect after 1724, defining the status of blacks as chattel, the evidence indicates that there was no real separation of the races and the slaves were generally treated as lesser members of the family. With an Anglo-Saxon change in style essentially the same arrangement prevailed over much of Arkansas in the territorial period.

The main streams of immigration initially flowed into the northern and western sections, so that by 1830 approximately 68 percent of the total population and 61 percent of the slaves lived in twelve counties classified as highland. All of these except Washington lay along navigable rivers and included fertile valleys. Here there were ready access to good land and a healthy climate, in contrast to areas along the lower Arkansas and the Mississippi plagued by floods and miasma. The usual land- and slaveholdings were small, and the crops were primarily for home consumption. In the years before the swampy flatlands were drained and cleared to permit large-scale cotton cultivation, Arkansas's leading farm products were grain, cattle, and hogs, the staples in the free territory to the north.

Charles Giles Bridle Daubeny, an Oxford professor of history

1. Orville W. Taylor, *Negro Slavery in Arkansas* (Durham: Duke University Press, 1958), p. 19.

and botany who toured the Arkansas backcountry in 1837–1838, described in his published *Journal* the sparse accommodations of a family recently arrived from Alabama, but noted that he was served a bountiful supper of coffee, cornbread, bacon, wild turkey, and venison, and concluded that his hosts "evidently lived better than persons of the same condition in England." In White County, Daubeny spent several days with the Walker family, describing its head as "one of the best specimens of an American yeoman, with somewhat of a Presbyterian cast about him. . . . No spirits were allowed to enter the house, a little circumstance alone sufficient to denote the difference between the Arkansas and the English farmer." The Walker place was some forty miles from Little Rock, with no village in between, and Daubeny was struck by the effect of this isolation:

> Where the negroes are chiefly employed in farming concerns, and are not numerous, the institution of slavery assumes something of a patriarchal character, and each proprietor may be regarded in the light of a country squire, having much time at his disposal, and exercising a species of feudal sway over his dependants.
>
> What land he cultivates yields abundant returns, without manure or previous preparation, but his chief support is derived from his hogs, which find subsistance mainly in the woods, and from his herds, which at one season are sent to fatten in the rich marshes near the Mississippi, and at another are brought back to the pastures nearer home. . . .
>
> The only unhospitable treatment I met was from the dogs, who, in a country so infested with wolves as this, are necessarily of a savage breed, or to use the queer expression of the country, very severe.[2]

So long as there were suitable lands to be had cheap east of the Mississippi, there was little compulsion for the more affluent planters to cast their lot in the Arkansas wilderness. Charles Sealsfield was not merely indulging in British snobbery when he toured the Mississippi Valley in 1828 and noted: "Arkansas has hitherto been the refuge for poor adventurers, foreigners, French soldiers, German redemptioners, with a few respectable American families; men of fortune preferred the state of Mississippi or

---

2. Margaret Ross, "Chronicles of Arkansas," *Arkansas Gazette*, Jan. 11, 1960.

Louisiana, where society and the comforts of life can be found with less difficulty." [3] In 1835 another foreign observer, Joseph Latrobe, seemed to agree on the matter of respectability but added another dimension: "Many a man, born and educated for better things, but who, living badly or freely in the old states, lastly mortgaging his estate and plunging irrevocably in debt, made over his debts to his older son, stole a horse, and off to Arkansas!" [4]

This background makes something less than a perfect fit with Frederick Jackson Turner's famous word picture in *The Rise of the New West* depicting the storied southern planter heading West to expand the domain of the Cotton Kingdom, traveling in state in his family carriage attended by servants, a pack of hunting dogs, and a train of slaves. In time a few such made it all the way to Arkansas, but they arrived late. Before the transmississippi could be declared a duchy of the slave empire, forests had to be cleared and Indians removed; as late as 1860 more than a third of Arkansas's acreage remained under federal title, with only 1,983,313 of its 9,473,706 acres listed by the census as improved.

The immigrants who first made their mark on the territory were likely to have been rambunctious opportunists on the order of Sam Houston, who abandoned his wife and the office of governor of Tennessee to undertake a protracted drunken sojourn in the Arkansas woods with his Cherokee friends. In 1830 the future president of the Lone Star Republic was running a trading post and writing letters to the *Gazette* berating Arkansans for selling whiskey to the Indians, while manfully admitting that he was "far from being a practically temperate man myself." [5] The editors of his autobiography wrote:

> It has been said that, after moving to Texas, Sam Houston often visited with his red brothers in Arkansas. When his fortunes permitted, he rode horseback; when he was broke, he walked.

3. Ross, "Chronicles of Arkansas," *Arkansas Gazette,* July 18, 1960.
4. Ross, "Chronicles of Arkansas," *Arkansas Gazette,* Oct. 12, 1960.
5. Donald Day and Harry Herbert Ullom, editors, *The Autobiography of Sam Houston* (Norman: University of Oklahoma Press, 1954), p. 62.

When he rode he made forty miles a day; when he walked, he made ten. The report was current that the course he took, and whether he rode or walked, could be traced out the next year by the half-blood babies that were spaced either forty or ten miles apart.[6]

This was Sam Houston at the nadir of his fortunes. At the zenith his style also was akin to that of many of Arkansas's founding fathers. In 1833 the man the Cherokee called "the Raven" rode into the state astride a splendid bay horse, his six-foot, six-inch frame draped in a richly ornamented Mexican poncho, his saddle and bridle worked with solid silver plates and buckles. One who beheld this imposing sight mistook him for a gambler—as indeed he was, although faro and seven-up were only minor diversions from the high-stakes game he was playing for the ultimate conquest of Texas. This Sam Houston was elegant of speech as well as of dress; he was a member of the bar, had been a major general of Tennessee militia, and had been appointed Indian agent for Arkansas on recommendation of his friend and sponsor, Andrew Jackson, only to reject the assignment when he made his successful race for governor.

Albert Pike was an outsize Arkansan of comparable attainments and equally spectacular style. A visiting correspondent who saw Pike in all his glory wrote: "He is somewhat eccentric in his dress, eschewing all conventional rules. . . . In fact he seems to delight in dressing in opposition to fashion. . . . His beard and moustaches are of most huge dimensions, while a heavy suit of hair hangs in masses on his neck and shoulder." [7]

At a stag party in 1852 Pike spun out a parody of an old English drinking song in honor of his friend, Maj. Elias Rector, a member of the prominent political family who had settled below Fort Smith. The ballad provides a not entirely satirical vignette of the less inhibited members of the society that came into being in the antebellum years:

Now all good fellows listen, and a story I will tell
Of a mighty clever gentleman who lives extremely well
In the Western part of Arkansas, close to the Indian line;

6. Day and Ullom, *Sam Houston,* p. xv.
7. Ross, "Chronicles of Arkansas," *Arkansas Gazette,* Sept. 28, 1958.

Where he gets drunk once a week on whiskey and immediately sobers
*   himself up completely on the very best wine.*
A fine Arkansas gentleman
Close to the Choctaw line!

Pike went on to celebrate Rector's custom of chartering a steamboat to take his cotton and his friends down the river to New Orleans, where his fame as a freespender was such that a leading hotel kept a silver plaque bearing his name on the door of his usual suite:

The last time he was down there, when he thought of going back,
After staying about fifteen days more or less, he discovered that by
lending and by spending, and by being a prey in general to
gamblers, hackmen, loafers, brokers, hosiers, tailors, servants and
many other individuals, white and black,
He had distributed his assets and got rid of all his means;
And had nothing left to show for them, barring two or three
headaches, an invincible thirst, and an extremely general and
promiscuous acquaintance in the aforesaid New Orleans;
This fine Arkansas gentleman,
Close to the Choctaw line! [8]

Not all the leading figures lived in such flamboyant style; the shoulder-length hair affected by Pike and his friend Rector was unusual to the point of eccentricity; and some of the most prominent men, notably William Woodruff, were conspicuous for their abstemiousness. Toward the close of the antebellum period the more prosperous planters would begin to find a place in this company, but the prosperous lawyer-politicians were still dominant. At Little Rock, Pine Bluff, Helena, Batesville, Fort Smith, Searcy, Camden, and Washington there emerged a fairly well-settled urban society, served by Hot Springs as a watering place. In the towns there began to appear lofty columned brick or frame houses, and the fine Arkansas gentlemen who moved along the streets wore broadcloth and dressed their ladies in ribboned bonnets.

In 1833, when the sheriff's census showed that the population had passed 40,000, thus rendering Arkansas eligible for

8. John Gould Fletcher, *Arkansas* (Chapel Hill: University of North Carolina Press, 1947), p. 125.

statehood, the political gentry generally opposed the move. To the Dynasty the prestige of full political status could hardly offset the loss of federal funds covering most of the cost of governance, these disbursed by its own members through their dominance of the territorial government. But upon his arrival at the next session of Congress, Ambrose Sevier, the Dynasty's man in Washington, reversed himself and introduced a resolution requesting authorization for a constitutional convention as the first step toward admission to the Union.

The about-face resulted from the movement of Michigan Territory for entry as a free state, which meant that a slave state had to be added to maintain the North-South balance. Arkansas was the South's obvious candidate for the trade-off, yet at that stage of the territory's development there was something less than unanimity on the underlying issue. In 1834, when the proponents of statehood began urging a constitutional convention upon the reluctant Gov. William S. Fulton, the lowland plantation belt was still in a rudimentary stage of development; the great majority of Arkansans had no vested interest in the "peculiar institution," and a substantial number thought they would be better off without it.

In the debate that followed the moral issue posed by slavery does not appear to have intruded at all. A resolution supporting statehood adopted at a public meeting in Jackson County conceded that it might have been better had this "species of property" never been introduced into the United States:

> But our slaves are now here. They have been entailed upon us by our ancestors. Our knowledge has been coeval with the possession and use of them; and whether they be to us a blessing or a curse, they have grown upon our hands, and involved our means and support to such an extent that now to rid ourselves of them, either by emancipation or colonization abroad, without encumbering ourselves with a still greater evil and incurring an insupportable loss, would be a thing impossible; at least a task which we are not willing, and which no human power can reasonably coerce upon us to bear.[9]

9. Taylor, *Negro Slavery in Arkansas,* p. 27.

About the only recorded opposition to statehood was confined to those who feared an increase in taxes. The controversy was colored by class antagonism between upcountry and low, as evidenced in this letter to the *Little Rock Times* in 1835:

> Of the whole white population, for one who has twenty slaves, we will find you twenty who have no slaves. The one, then will be the sufferer by the abolition of slavery in the Territory, and to enable him to loll in ease and affluence, and to save his own delicate hands from the rude contact of the vulgar plow, the twenty who earn their honest living by the sweat of the brow are called upon with the voice of authority assumed by wealth to receive the yoke. They must consent to a tenfold increase of tax for the support of a state government, because my lord is threatened with danger of desertion from his cotton field if we remain as we are.
>
> To this the nonslaveholders who compose, as will appear by the new census, an overwhelming majority of the territory, cannot submit. They are willing to forego the advantages to *themselves* of the abolition of slavery . . . but a greater sacrifice cannot, in justice, be expected.[10]

Nevertheless, the greater sacrifice was to be exacted, for from that time forward the special interest of the slaveholders would be paramount in the politics of antebellum Arkansas.

The slave population grew rapidly as the fertile lowlands were cleared and broken for cotton. Arkansas had 1,617 blacks in 1820, nearly 20,000 in 1840, and 111,115 at the zenith of the slave system in 1860; but the white population was growing too, and, although the proportion of blacks to whites rose from census to census the slave population never exceeded 25 percent. Only six counties, all deep in the plantation belt, counted blacks a majority, and in much of the upland area beyond the river valleys they were never more than a trace. In 1860 the 11,481 slaveowners amounted only to 3.5 percent of the white population, and more than half of these had title to less than four.

It is generally agreed that at least twenty slaves were required

---

10. Taylor, *Negro Slavery in Arkansas,* p. 38.

to maintain an establishment that by the most modest standard could qualify as a plantation. By this criterion the 1850 census recorded only 524 plantations in Arkansas, with their owners confined to 1.6 percent of the population; of these only 127 were major operations with more than fifty slaves. By 1860 the number of plantations had increased to 1,070, but their proprietors still accounted for only 9 percent of the slaveholding population. The size of individual holdings had grown significantly; 279 planters now owned more than 50, 59 more than a 100, 6 more than 200, and 1 had more than 500. These were major commercial enterprises representing a heavy capital investment in land and labor.

At the other end of the scale, Orville W. Taylor, in his *Negro Slavery in Arkansas,* concluded that half the slaveowners, the 5,806 holding four slaves or fewer, did not regard their human chattel as revenue-producing. These were cooks, maids, houseboys, gardeners, stableboys, nurses, and extra hands on small farms. The ultimate of this kind of personal service was enjoyed by Chester Ashley, whose town house stood in the middle of a city block in Little Rock and was maintained by a black domestic staff that included seven males who played brass and string instruments well enough to give frequent concerts on the broad front lawn. The 12,131 blacks in this servant class were to be found in all parts of Arkansas except the more remote mountain areas, but they accounted for only 11 percent of the total.

Another 43 percent of the slaves lived and worked on farms too small to be classed as plantations. Taylor concluded that these 48,000 agricultural laborers returned a profit to their owners and were essential to their farm operations. This productivity is reflected in the marked rise in agricultural wealth between 1850 and 1860, when the cash value of farms increased from $15,265,245 to $91,649,773. The increase was accounted for in part by the fourfold increase in cultivated land as settlers pushed into new country, but the average farm acreage also rose from 146 to 245, and the average value per farm from $893 to $2,349. Some idea of how this valuation might break down in the case of small farmers is given by Taylor, who found that in 1853 in Union County his great-great-grandfather's three slaves were valued at $2,000, while a 320-acre farm, horse, and ten cows had a total value of only $1,400.

In the case of the major planters the disproportion in the value of slaves and land is demonstrated by the record of James Sheppard. In 1839 the young William and Mary graduate was the $800-a-year manager of a plantation owned by his father, a Richmond physician, in Copiah County, Mississippi. In 1847 James and his brother bought out their father's interest, giving him a note for $36,000—the bulk of the payment representing the value of 100 slaves at an average price of $300. In 1851 Sheppard rented out his holdings in Mississippi and moved his slaves to Waterford Plantation near Pine Bluff, where he paid $20,000 for 1,017 acres. In 1860 he bought nearby Blenheim Plantation, paying $60 an acre for the land and $1,250 a head for forty-six slaves. Rising prices for land and slaves, plus canny reinvestment, increased Sheppard's original capital of $3,000 more than fiftyfold, while enabling him to live quite well off the proceeds.

Thus, in fifteen years a young man who owned practically nothing had become wealthy by any contemporary American standard. However, if Sheppard started with little capital of his own he had the equivalent in access to his father's credit. Few were able to work their way up from scratch in the plantation business; if unimproved land could be had cheap on the frontier, slaves could not, and gang labor was an inescapable requirement of the money crop.

In 1860 a young Englishman, Henry Morton Stanley, later to be knighted for his discoveries in Africa, including Dr. Livingston, was present at the genesis of a plantation in Saline County. Arriving from New Orleans with his host, a Major Ingham, he found the numerous slaves engaged in pushing back the forest wall. Stanley pitched in to help, working alongside the blacks as they felled the tall pines and cut them into chunks to feed the bonfires that disposed of them. It was, Stanley found, a sort of team contest accompanied by singing and chanting. "They appeared to enjoy it," he wrote in his *Autobiography,* "and the atmosphere, laden with the scent of burning resin, the roaring fires, the dance of the lively flames, the excitement of the gangs while holding on, with grim resolve and honor bound, to the bearing spikes, had a real fascination for me." [11]

Nor did the organized effort to bring in "new ground" end with the initial clearing. The stumps had to be burned or grubbed out, and periodically the fields had to be "scrubbed" of new sprouts. Years elapsed before a cottonfield carved out of the forest provided the smooth, unbroken expanse of rich land essential to efficient cultivation.

In recent years revisionist historians have reopened the long-standing argument over the presumed profitability of the slave-based plantation system. Whether or not slavery contained, as some argue, the seeds of its own ultimate economic destruction, it simply swept all other considerations aside in the years when it came to dominate the new states absorbed into the Cotton Kingdom. "Insofar as Arkansas was concerned," Taylor wrote, "the author agrees, in general, with those writers who have contended that slavery was profitable." [12] However, he conceded that this may have been true only where conditions were favorable for the use of gang labor on large holdings—that is, in the dozen counties where plantations were concentrated.

The issue of slave profitability leaves open the question whether the peculiar institution ever was, or ever could have been, beneficial to the great majority of Arkansas's white population. The 1,363 plantations in Arkansas in 1860 compare with 5,895 in Mississippi; 3,895 in Louisiana; 2,932 in Tennessee; and 2,163 in Texas. Proportionately this would seem to place the state's economic interests closer to those Border States which stayed with the Union, than to those of its secessionist neighbors.

W. J. Cash noted the cultural implications of this economic pattern in *The Mind of the South*. The Cotton Kingdom simply did not survive long enough to develop on a large scale the kind of established plantation gentry whose seaboard prototype he labeled Virginian. Cash calculated that the claim to southern-style aristocracy required two or more generations of recognized

11. Taylor, *Negro Slavery in Arkansas*, p. 95.
12. Taylor, *Negro Slavery in Arkansas*, p. 121.

status and affluence. Few families with such pretensions were personally engaged in opening the new territory west of the Mississippi. Little more than a single generation elapsed before the dream of a slave empire came to an abrupt end: "It was actually 1820 before the plantation was fully on the march, striding over the hills of Carolina to Mississippi—1820 before the tide of immigration was in full sweep around the base of the Appalachians." [13] That tide would not reach flood stage in Arkansas until the last two decades before the Civil War.

Francis Butler Simkins, the South Carolina–born historian, notes that few of the original planters in the new cotton states made any claim to the Cavalier antecedents so admired by the Virginians. The majority were self-made men, of the same blood as their more humble neighbors, set apart initially only by their superior energy: "Theirs was an aristocracy with a yeoman background and without heraldic devices. Such men had little time to be ostentatious, leaving to descendants the creation of the Southern myth." [14]

Nevertheless, Arkansas's conversion to the Confederate cause was no more reluctant than that of other states of the upper South. This can only be explained in theological terms, as a matter of faith if not necessarily of morals. In the light of contemporary experience, which demonstrates that the racial manifestation of man's inhumanity to man hardly can be isolated on a regional basis, it is difficult to take seriously the abolitionist contention that the ordinarily devout slaveholders were guilty of a unique form of original sin. More to the point was the fact that the vast majority of the settlers, whether planters or yeomen, arrived already conditioned by the mores of the southern colonial commonwealths. Slavery to them was of the natural order of things; they had never known blacks in any other condition.

"Slavery was close to the heart of the peculiar social practices of the Old South," Simkins has written. "The relation between master and slave had the sanction of habit and custom; it was invested with a sanctity similar to that bestowed upon the

13. W. J. Cash, *The Mind of the South* (New York: Alfred A. Knopf, 1941), p. 10.

14. Francis Butler Simkins, *The South Old and New* (New York: Alfred A. Knopf, 1947), p. 51.

relation between parent and child." [15] Whether it was the product of a tender heart or a practical mind a sort of imposed paternalism was essential to the plantation system; the typical holding was isolated by the broad acreage required to produce the money crop, and an effective degree of social unity was implicit in any successful planter's operation.

This was true whether the plantation was a storied place of white columns, rosy brick, and spreading lawns, or, as was usually the case, a collection of modest one-story structures weathering to silver gray on a stretch of bare earth swarming with white and black children, dogs, chickens, and pigs. There was necessarily a sense of community here; if the blacks were not present by choice, it nevertheless was the only home they had.

Black field hands may have worked harder and longer than did poor whites on their hillside farms, and certainly they were subject to calculated degradation, but their level of subsistence and creature comfort was at least equal—if for no other reason because their health and morale were key factors in an operation that involved a capital investment at a going rate of up to $1,500 for a prime field hand. Even those owners who engaged in the not-uncommon practice of renting out their slaves for gang labor on river and road improvement projects were careful to see that their valuable property was not abused. No doubt there were some inhuman overseers, but they did not work for prudent proprietors.

As Arkansas began to attain a more settled character planters came to prominence whose probity could hardly have been questioned by the most rigorous abolitionist on any ground other than support of the peculiar institution. One of these, Colin McRae of North Carolina, founded the community of Mount Holly in Union County near the Louisiana border.

McRae arrived in 1843, accompanied by "several families of African slaves," and began clearing land bought from the government at prices ranging up to $1.25 an acre. By the end of the year he had brought on from Carolina a dozen or more relatives,

15. Simkins, *The South Old and New,* p. 54.

described by a devoted descendant, Samuel H. Chester, as a "sturdy tribe, noted for business sagacity, incorruptible integrity, and the absence of any fear complex in their psychological makeup." [16] As the Mount Holly community grew the roll call of incoming planters had the ring of a Scot reunion: Buckner, Chester, Wright, Morgan, Strawn, Lewis, Crisp, Parker, McCall, Smead.

It was the first order of business for such as these to establish a Presbyterian church, and soon thereafter an academy. Chester describes the Old Field School as a "kind of log college," and the preparation he received there was sufficient to relieve him of any embarrassment upon his matriculation at Washington College in Virginia shortly after the Civil War, when Robert E. Lee was that institution's president.

As the McRaes and their in-laws brokered the land they wrote prohibition clauses into the deeds, and Chester deduced that this was a prime reason no permanent resident of Mount Holly was ever convicted of a felony within his memory. He testified that he did not lay eyes on a drunken man until the second year of the Civil War, when he was twelve years old and there were strangers in the neighborhood. The contrast between this austere society and the gaudy world of the Fine Arkansas Gentlemen is implicit in Chester's memoir, *Pioneer Days in Arkansas,* written in 1927 when he had become secretary emeritus of foreign missions for the Presbyterian Church in the United States.

The tone of the social life is indicated in Chester's description of the ordinary discourse among his relatives and neighbors: "Their English was that of the King James Bible, and the topics they discussed were those connected with the history and literature of their day." [17] Chester's father, a physician who married Colin McRae's sister, maintained a library that included the works of Macaulay, Hume, and Gibbon, with Scott, Jane Austen, Hawthorne, Lamb, and Shakespeare available for entertainment.

The Chester family owned a dozen slaves, and some of the

---

16. Samuel H. Chester, *Pioneer Days in Arkansas* (Richmond: Presbyterian Committee on Publication, 1927), p. 12.

17. Chester, *Pioneer Days in Arkansas,* p. 15.

full-time planters in the community acquired as many as thirty or forty. In his summing-up, Samuel, the staunch Calvinist, conceded that "all intelligent Southerners are glad that it is sixty years behind us," but left this judgment for posterity: "I have no apology for the institution of slavery as it existed in the South before the Civil War." [18]

The McRae clan fulfilled Simkins's dictum that the descendants of the first wave of yeoman settlers would go on to fill in the visible dimensions of the southern myth. In 1903, K. B. McRae, born at Mount Holly in 1862 and a brother of Arkansas's Gov. Thomas C. McRae, moved to the town of Hope and built a mansion with a massive, two-story, columned portico. When this handsome establishment was placed on the National Register of Historic Places in 1976 it was noted that "the house has eleven bedrooms, each twenty-two feet square. The interior of the house includes a center hall with double parlors on each side. All woodwork is of fine-grained oak." [19]

The values that shaped the self-contained plantation society were inherited, and they survived despite their contrast with the harsh actuality of day-to-day existence. In 1860, when the generation sired within the state began approaching half the total population, the composition of the basic stock had been set, and the proportions would not change significantly in the century to come. Ninety-nine percent of the 324,335 whites were of American birth (as, for that matter, were the 111,115 blacks), and 97 percent were born in the South. The foreign-born included 1,312 Irish, 1,143 Germans, and a scattering of others.

The experience of Arkansas demonstrates that the mystique of the Old South was hardy enough to survive, and may very well have been enhanced by, the process of natural selection that brought these men and women to the frontier. Pioneering is a ruthlessly Darwinian process. Even those who came as refugees—from the law, from economic privation, or from some unendurable personal travail—had already demonstrated the will and capacity for action. Varied as they were in background, in

18. Chester, *Pioneer Days in Arkansas,* p. 38.
19. *Arkansas Gazette,* July 19, 1976.

temperament, and in capacity, all had one thing in common: They were looking for the main chance.

But in addition to the ambitious ones who measured progress in financial or at least material terms, a minority of practically inarticulate settlers carved out patch farms in the loneliest stretches of back country that represented no improvement on those they had left behind, and never would. What, then, was the main chance sought by the mountaineers who found their place among the long ridges of the Ozarks and the Ouachitas?

Since they rarely spoke for themselves, not at least in the conventional ways that provide the basis for the historical record, we have to rely on artists to divine what they were about. In his novel, *The Architecture of the Arkansas Ozarks,* a marvelously skewed history in parable form, Donald Harington gives us the explanation of Jacob Ingledew, who comes on scene "tall, dressed in buckskin jacket and trousers, wearing a headpiece made from the skin and tail of a raccoon, thin, blue-eyed, brown-haired, long-nosed, carrying not a rifle but a half-gallon jug with corncob stopper." Jacob has made a hard passage of six hundred miles from Warren County, Tennessee, to squat on land occupied by an Osage named Fanshaw. The Indian took his name and learned his English from a passing British explorer and has a weakness for philosophical discourse:

"It don't matter to me whether the earth is round or flat," Jacob said to Fanshaw . . . "I ain't gonna git to the other side nohow."

"Where *are* you going to get to, old chap?"

"Huh? I've done got there."

"The time has come, now, when we must at last cultivate a topic of discussion which, hitherto, we have avoided: why did you come here and build upon this land?"

"Hit was gitting jist too durn crowded back in Tennessee," Jacob said. "I purt near couldn't lift my elbow 'thout hittin somebody and the preachers was so thick a feller couldn't say 'heck' without gittin a sermon fer it."

"But you have never even asked for permission to build here. Stay More is the land of my grandfathers . . ."

Jacob Ingledew repeated the name a couple of times and himself chuckled. "I reckon that will do as well as ary other name."

"But you cannot," Fanshaw said.

"Cannot what?"

"Stay more."

"Says who?" Jacob demanded. "You fixin to try to run me off?"

"My grandfathers are buried here."

"My grandchildren will be buried here."

The passing of the years, and the working of Harington's antic imagination, take Jacob to a fictional governor's mansion in Little Rock in the aftermath of the Civil War. There, lying in bed looking up at the four-cornered ceiling of his bedroom, he suddenly jabs his elbow into his wife's ribs: "That's the trouble, Sarey! We've done went and boxed ourself in!" Sarah doesn't understand him, nor do those who see the mountaineers only as archaic, mildly comic figures on a remote landscape. The tragedy that underlies Harington's comedy is that for more than a century Jacob and his kind have been fated to "go on forever dwelling in boxes of various shapes and sizes.[20]

20. Donald Harington, *The Architecture of the Arkansas Ozarks* (Boston: Little Brown and Co., 1975), pp. 1, 16.

7

The Road to Secession

*T*HE first quarter-century of statehood is generally reckoned the most prosperous period Arkansas has known up to
modern times. Nostalgia no doubt put a gloss on the epoch, giving it, as John Gould Fletcher suggested, some of the dimensions of the sustaining southern myth that later generations
would cherish in the bitter days to come. It was, in any case, a
busy time that changed the harsh lineaments of frontier society.

As transportation improved and the state began to pull itself
together, the planters and yeoman farmers established communication with the towns that were linked commercially to the
world at large. On the rivers, which would remain the prime
movers for freight until the railroads belatedly traversed Arkansas in the 1870s, steamboats began to replace hand-propelled
keelboats early in the century. The first of these, the *Comet,*
docked at Arkansas Post in 1820, and two years later the *Eagle*
hove to at Little Rock. For most of the year the Arkansas was
navigable to Fort Smith, the White to a point above Batesville,
and service was also available on the Red and the Ouachita.
At about the same time stagecoaches came into regular service.

Because the state was, by present census standards, almost
100 percent rural, the principal towns, mostly situated on the
waterways, sustained a somewhat more substantial and complex
level of activity than the bare population figures suggest. In

1860 the census ranking was Little Rock, 3,727; Camden, 2,219; Fort Smith, 1,530; Pine Bluff, 1,396; and Fayetteville, 967. Only four other towns registered more than 500: Van Buren, Arkadelphia, Batesville, and Searcy. Yet, as early as 1832 Washington Irving, passing through Little Rock, was impressed by the fact that the village maintained two newspapers and three taverns. In 1834 an English traveler, George William Featherstonhaugh, attended a Christmas party at one of these, where about a hundred guests danced while armed to the teeth but, as he noted with relief, fired only a few shots, and these in fun. Horseracing and theatrical performances were regularly scheduled in the capital city in the late thirties.

By 1840, although the population was only about 1,500, it included persons from almost every state in the Union and several foreign countries; Little Rock was now adorned with large and impressive buildings, and such imported delicacies as oysters, bananas, pineapples, and citrus fruits were regularly available. Advertisements in the *Gazette* included one inserted by Jonas Levy that offered the services of a local fire insurance agency.

River traffic grew steadily; in 1859, from November until June when low water began to disrupt the schedule, there were 317 steamboat dockings at Little Rock, an average of more than one a day. Travelers now had access to an elegant three-story brick hotel, the Anthony House, with two parlors, a bar, and a dining room sixty feet long. By 1860 the town could boast a twenty-year-old federal arsenal, a college, a female seminary, what claimed to be the largest flour mill west of the Mississippi, a sprawling farmers' market surrounded by wagon yards, and gas lights. There were three newspapers, and the *True Democrat* began daily publication when the telegraph line came in from Memphis in 1861, as did the *Times and Herald* at Fort Smith, where the Morse wire came down from Missouri.

It was here in the towns that the critical political decisions were being made. Those who made them necessarily would be influenced by interaction with those who lived on the land, and, from the beginning of statehood, by the ideological currents flowing from the national centers of powers. These forces combined with the osmosis of inherited tradition to make Arkansas part of the Cotton Kingdom.

Prior to the climactic events of 1860 a considerable proportion of Arkansans believed that the Union should be preserved. But this Unionist sentiment was never manifest in significant opposition to the peculiar institution; if some leaders took issue with some aspects of the elaborate ideology evolved by southern politicians to justify the plantation system, no Arkansan of consequence arose to challenge the practice of holding black men in bondage.

There were outspoken abolitionists among the missionaries who came down from New England to work among the Indians, but the first of these, Cephas Washburn, made a clear distinction between the Christian obligations due red men and black. He could bring down a terrible wrath upon the head of a fellow clergyman involved in the Indian removal policies of the government: "The Cherokees hold you responsible; so do the people of the United States; so does the Church of God; so does the civilized world; and so does the Judge of all. The stain it fixes upon you, as a minister, as a Christian, as a man, is black and indellible." [1] But the Reverend J. W. Moore, the unreconstructed southern Presbyterian who wrote a biographical preface to Washburn's *Reminiscences,* testified that the old missionary manifested a preabolitionist strain of Puritanism:

> The theology of Jonathan Edwards and Timothy Dwight still held sway. . . . The Beechers and Cheevers and Garrisons had not then risen up to scatter the seeds of error and infidelity broadcast over the land. . . . When speaking of the fearful strides of fanaticism and infidelity, as recently developed in the land of his fathers, he was often heard to say that Congregationalism had not power sufficient to keep out heresy. [2]

There was a minor antislavery eruption among the Arkansas Methodists, referred to as the "Haile storm." The Reverend Jesse Haile, who served briefly as presiding elder in 1824–1825, took literally his denomination's social gospel and attempted to enforce the church's decree that none of its ordained ministers could own slaves. There was an immediate protest that this

---

1. Rev. Cephas Washburn, A.M., *Reminiscences of the Indians* (Richmond: Presbyterian Committee of Publication, 1869), p. 64.

2. Washburn, *Reminiscences of the Indians,* pp. 65, 66.

would deprive the Methodist clergy of its best minds, and the storm quickly subsided, along with Brother Haile. In 1845 the tenth session of the Arkansas Methodist Conference, assembled at Camden, formally declared the master-servant relationship in the slaveholding states "not necessarily sinful or a moral evil." The conference went on to announce "solemn preference for, and our determination strictly to adhere to, the Methodist Church, South." [3] Sectional cleavage now affected all the major Protestant churches.

The other leading denomination, the Baptist, at its state convention at Tulip in 1854 dealt with the slavery issue by exhorting "Christian masters to the faithful discharge of the fearful duties growing out of this situation. Give your servants that which is just and equal, knowing that you also have a master in heaven." The Baptists, who permitted black Christians to worship in segregated galleries in their churches, also urged the planters to support an increased missionary effort, "knowing that religion makes slaves industrious, temperate, honest and obedient." [4]

Injection of the moral issue into the continuing sectional controversy served to unite Arkansas's divided constituency. The brand of racial justice espoused in the North had the effect of triggering what the southern historian Frank Vandiver calls an offensive-defense mechanism.

Ambrose Sevier's argument in favor of the constitutional convention that would make Arkansas a slave state was an exercise in undiluted chauvinism. He warned his fellow citizens that there was "a battle to fight with fanaticism upon the subject of slavery. . . . Our rights are secured to us by the third article of the treaty of April 30, 1803. They are secured to us by the constitution itself. Our ancestors tired of colonial vassalage, and so have we." [5]

The most moderate political view voiced in Arkansas, usually by the Whigs, rested on the assumption that those in the North

3. Orville W. Taylor, *Negro Slavery in Arkansas* (Durham: Duke University Press, 1958), p. 175.

4. Taylor, *Negro Slavery in Arkansas,* p. 169.

5. Taylor, *Negro Slavery in Arkansas,* p. 36.

who inveighed against slavery acted not in malice but in ignorance. This was not simply a manifestation of frontier parochialism. In an 1836 issue of the *American Monthly Magazine* the erudite Albert Pike, Massachusetts born and educated, patrician by predilection if not by birth, active supporter of Henry Clay's nationalist policies, addressed himself in sorrow to the Yankee companions of his youth:

> . . . every movement of the abolitionists is riveting the fetters on the limbs of the Negro—heating them red hot, and scorching them in—increasing his daily task—narrowing down his measure of comfort and relaxation—and exposing him oftener to the lash. Why? Because it increases the suspicion in the planter, and renders new strictness and security necessary; yea, gives excuse to severity. . . . [I tell them] their schemes are impractible—that the Negroes cannot be liberated—that if they could it would produce a war of extermination, resulting in the absolute extinction of the slaves—I tell them too, that the greatest curse you can inflict on a slave is to free him.[6]

Another northern import, who opposed Pike on most local and national issues, shared these convictions. William Woodruff was particularly concerned about the incendiary effect of abolitionist propaganda, and the columns of the *Gazette* reflected his obsession with what he regarded as the potential danger of a slave insurrection. He demanded that the postmaster general suppress the circulation of antislavery literature, and forthrightly urged lynching for abolitionist agitators of any color, although there is no hard evidence that any such ever were active in the state.

By July 1858, the conspiracy phobia had become so prevalent a group of leading citizens issued a circular urging expatriation of all free blacks, arguing that "even if they do nothing actively, their very existence here and their condition as free men, make them constant, though silent preachers to the slave, of notions that are dangerous in the last degree to us, and injurious to him." [7] In February 1859, the legislature passed a law requiring all free blacks to leave the state by the end of the year; those

6. Margaret Ross, "Chronicles of Arkansas," *Arkansas Gazette,* Aug. 24, 1960.
7. Ross, "Chronicles of Arkansas," *Arkansas Gazette,* Feb. 15, 1960.

who remained after the deadline had the option of being impounded by the county and hired out for twelve months, with a portion of their wage used to provide them with travel funds, or of voluntarily choosing masters and becoming slaves again. Since the 1858 sheriff's census showed 682 freedmen, and the 1860 census only 144, the measure appears to have been effective.

The great national schism came to dominate state politics. When Martin Van Buren made common cause with the free-soilers in 1848 a bill was introduced in the Arkansas Senate to change the name of Van Buren County; Andy Jackson's political heir was declared guilty of "adhering to abolitionist fanatics, giving them aid and comfort in their treasonable crusade against the South." [8] Arkansas gave a majority to the proslavery Democratic ticket headed by Lewis Cass, but only by a narrow margin of some two thousand more than the 7,582 votes cast for the nationally victorious Whig ticket headed by Zachary Taylor.

Both parties were being fragmented by the slavery issue, and by 1854 a new political movement was arising among the splintered factions. The American party's adherents were identified as Know-Nothings because of their lodge-style oath requiring that they profess ignorance if questioned by outsiders about the party's inner workings. There were religious overtones in the nativist thesis that immigrants, who were largely Roman Catholic, should be barred from participation in government and otherwise treated as second-class citizens. This was not, however, a simple appeal to bigotry; in the North the Know-Nothings drew their strength from workers who quite reasonably feared that the flood of cheap immigrant labor would hold down their wages; in the South, where immigrants were few, the American party became a refuge for pro-Union moderates who were trying to head off the firebrand states' rights Democrats, before whom they stood disarmed on the issue of slavery.

In Arkansas leading Whigs, including Albert Pike and Absalom Fowler, declared as Know-Nothings, and a movement

8. Ross, "Chronicles of Arkansas," *Arkansas Gazette,* July 6, 1960.

started to bring out a new party organ to replace the defunct *Arkansas Whig*. Ironically, one of the new owners, John Milton Butler, was killed in a gun battle on the street with his brother-in-law, Edward Marcus—whose antagonism to the Know-Nothing cause was explained by the fact that he was himself a German immigrant. As a result the Know-Nothing banner was passed on to the *Gazette,* which had been sold again by Woodruff and was now under the editorship of the volatile Solon Borland, retired from the Senate and back in Little Rock after a controversial diplomatic career in Central America.

In the 1856 election the national Democratic ticket headed by James Buchanan carried Arkansas handily, while the Know-Nothing gubernatorial candidate, James Yell, was defeated by the Dynasty's Elias Conway, 27,612 to 15,249. John William Brown, a prosperous Camden lawyer, land speculator, and planter, wrote an epitaph for Whiggery in Arkansas after he backed Absalom Fowler—"a firm, consistent, conservative, union-loving man"—in an unsuccessful race for Congress against Col. Edward A. Warren—"a mere party hack and a blustering pot-house politician." Brown despaired for the Republic:

> The sovereign cry of Democrat seems to be sweeping everything before and I . . . am satisfied that if some providential change does not take place, our Union cannot stand five years longer—and whenever the Union is dissolved there is an end to all safety in the rights of property, or security for its peaceful professions.[9]

As this curious force for moderation passed into a footnote to the nation's and the state's history, the political realignment continued, with the factions in Arkansas bearing prefixes to qualify their partisan commitment. Among the contending newspapers there was now a *True Democrat* and an *Old Line Democrat*. The talk of secession was growing, but unionist sentiment continued strong through the fateful election of 1860. Arkansas gave the uncompromising proslavery ticket headed by

9. Horace Adams, "Diary of an Arkansas Whig," *Arkansas Historical Quarterly* 1 (Summer 1941):131.

ARKANSAS

A photographer's essay by A. Y. Owen

John C. Breckinridge of Kentucky 28,732 votes, but 20,094 voted for John Bell of Tennessee, who declared for conditional preservation of the Union, and another 5,227 stayed with the regular Democrats headed by Stephen A. Douglas.

In that last testing of national sentiment before the outbreak of war Abraham Lincoln, the ex-Whig who won the presidency, had no electors on the ballot in Arkansas. Public opinion had become so polarized it simply was not possible for Arkansans to consider the candidacy of the man from Illinois who was so close to many of them in background and temperament, and in his pragmatic view of the slavery issue.

Temporizing political leaders went down before the increasing militancy. Henry M. Rector, dissident planter-member of the old reigning family, defeated the Dynasty's candidate for governor, and an uncompromising states' righter from Eastern Arkansas, Thomas C. Hindman of Helena, who would soon wear the stars of a Confederate general, now sat in Congress. In his inaugural address on November 15, 1860, Governor Rector in effect called for secession, declaring that the issue had been forced by the North to the point where it now must be defined as the Union without slavery, or slavery without the Union. In December South Carolina announced her independence, to be followed by Florida, Georgia, Louisiana, and Texas, and in February 1861, the Confederate States of America came into being at Montgomery. In a special election Arkansas voted 27,472 to 15,826 in favor of a convention to consider secession. War fever was running, and under pressure from avid volunteer militia groups Governor Rector called for and received surrender of the Federal arsenal at Little Rock.

But when the convention assembled on March 4, 1861, it promptly elected an antisecessionist chairman, David Walker, a Washington County Whig leader, and over the next two weeks, by margins that narrowed to 39–35, voted down all efforts to align Arkansas with the Confederacy. Governor Rector confronted the delegates with the question the unionists sought to avoid: "Does there exist inside the borders of Arkansas any diversity of sentiment as to the religious or moral right of holding negro slaves?'' [10] The answer quite clearly was no, but still a majority held out, and the convention adjourned after referring the matter of secession to a special election called for the following August.

The internal political division in Arkansas disappeared after a handful of gray-clad South Carolinians fired on Fort Sumter in Charleston harbor. Three days later, on April 15, President Lincoln called on the state to provide troops to suppress the insurrection, and Governor Rector replied with what amounted to a declaration of independence:

> In answer to your requisition for troops from Arkansas to subjugate the Southern states I have to say that none will be furnished. The demand is only adding insult to injury. The people of this commonwealth are freemen, not slaves, and will defend to the last extremity their honor, lives and property against Northern mendacity and usurpation.[11]

On May 6 the convention reassembled and on the first ballot voted 65–5 for secession. After a call to make the vote unanimous only one dissenting vote stood, that of Isaac Murphy of remote Madison County in the Ozarks. Murphy's lonely act of courage was saluted by a bouquet of flowers floating down from the gallery where the townspeople had assembled to see history made. And many of those who voted for secession carried their doubts away with them. ''Our people are thoroughly imbued with the revolutionary spirit,'' the Van Buren Whig leader, Jesse Turner, wrote to his wife Rebecca. ''Madness and folly rule the land and I fear that the end of free government approaches. The conservative men who were for the union cannot stay the rushing tide of revolution.'' [12]

The war did not wait for these formalities. On April 21 Governor Rector had dispatched four companies of volunteers upriver in three steamboats to capture the Federal garrison at

10. David Y. Thomas, *Arkansas in War and Reconstruction* (Little Rock: United Daughters of the Confederacy, 1926), p. 79.

11. John Gould Fletcher, *Arkansas* (Chapel Hill: University of North Carolina Press, 1947), pp. 146, 147.

12. George H. Thompson, *Arkansas and Reconstruction* (Port Washington, N.Y.: Kennikat Press, 1976), p. 34.

Fort Smith. Upon their approach the regular army troops decamped and the victorious, if unblooded, expedition proceeded back down the Arkansas. One of the young blades wrote: "Cheering was the order of the day, on shore and aboard. Artillery salutes and brass bands wore out all ears, patience, and 'Dixie.' By order we had two field pieces on the forecastle, firing salutes, which left a stink of sulfur and saltpeter, and a ribbon of smoke, from Belle Pointe to Petit Rocher." [13] So, with a rebel yell, Arkansas rallied to the Stars and Bars; by September 20,000 men had volunteered, although there were only arms on hand for 10,000.

13. Fletcher, *Arkansas,* p. 147.

8

War Comes to Arkansas

*T*HERE was more to Arkansas's overwhelming, if belated, response to the Confederacy's call to arms than the glamor and spontaneous excitement of a war that had not yet begun to exact its penalties. Those who rushed forward to fill the ranks thought of themselves as patriots, and by any test they were; reservations about the wisdom of the political judgments involved did not relieve them of their duty; the Union was gone now, and Arkansas was their country. Susan Bricelin Fletcher, a matriarch of the remarkable clan still prominent in the state, wrote of her husband and his five brothers: "Four enlisted at once, notwithstanding the fact that they believed that to secede from the United States was a mistake, and to begin the new Confederacy with a new flag a greater one, if possible. Their father had fought in 1812, and their grandfather in 1776." [1]

Men of every degree and from all sections of the state flocked to the colors. Two hundred companies were mustered in 1861. At Mount Ida, in the hills back of Hot Springs, a hundred men came forward armed with old flintlock rifles and double-barrel shotguns. There was a homemade drum and a fife made of cane to provide martial music, and two ox wagons to haul the company's bed quilts, pots, skillets, and pans. *Historic Arkansas* said of the Mount Ida volunteers, "Not a man in the company

---

1. Margaret Ross, "Chronicles of Arkansas," *Arkansas Gazette,* Aug. 28, 1966.

knew anything about military tactics, and most of them would never come back.'' [2]

If they were ignorant of the martial arts they had the qualities that would distinguish one of the most remarkable armies ever to lose a war: they could shoot, they could march, they could endure any weather, and they would stand and fight. Most of the able-bodied men in Arkansas—60,000 out of a white population of only 324,000—wore Confederate gray; another 9,000, mostly from the northwest counties, enlisted in the Union army; and more than 5,000 blacks were under arms after the Federal occupying forces organized four regiments of Arkansas Volunteers of African Descent.

Two Arkansas regiments were with Robert E. Lee's Army of Northern Virginia before the end of 1861. Col. Albert Rust's Third Arkansas Infantry served in the Shenandoah with Stonewall Jackson's "foot cavalry," and went on to Malvern Hill, Gettysburg, the Wilderness, Cold Harbor, and Petersburg; at Appomattox the Third Arkansas stacked only 300 rifles of the 1,500 borne by its men ten months before. There were Arkansas units in all the bloody battles in Kentucky and Tennessee, and their tattered remnants were with Joe Johnston when he finally capitulated to William Tecumseh Sherman in North Carolina. The state's most distinguished Confederate commander, Maj. Gen. Patrick R. Cleburne of Helena, was credited with saving the Army of Tennessee at Missionary Ridge, and probably would have succeeded to its command had he not been killed in action at the Battle of Franklin in late 1864.

Glory on the eastern front was soon to be matched by bitterness at home. In the first year of the war there was a possibility that Arkansas might become a key battleground as both the Union and Confederate commands stumbled through their early efforts at organization and tactical planning. It could be assumed that the Federal forces would try a major thrust southward from Missouri, where the secession movement had failed although the governor and other state officials had declared for the Confederacy. Control of the Mississippi River would split off the southwestern states and isolate the Confederacy from a major source of grain and cattle to supply its armies, and of cotton to maintain critical trade with foreign markets. In the end the troops under Ulysses Grant were ordered to make the main effort through the Mississippi Valley, but initially the Southern commanders had good reason to fear a flanking movement through Bloody Kansas and the Indian Territory.

Arkansas had anticipated its vulnerability. At the secession convention E. C. Boudinot, a half-breed Cherokee lawyer, served as secretary, and Albert Pike was dispatched forthwith to the territory with the mission of enlisting support of the 65,000 Indians colonized on the reservations of the Five Civilized Tribes. He negotiated treaties under which the Indian nations allied themselves with the Confederacy, a task eased by the fact that most of the tribal leaders themselves were slaveowners: the 1860 census recorded 14,638 slaves in the territory, a proportion comparable to that in Arkansas. The abolitionist missionaries who founded the Indian schools had been declared persona non grata, and Annie Heloise Abel, who wrote a massive three-volume history of the Indian Territory's involvement in the Civil War, concluded: "The Holy See itself could never have been more vigilant in protecting colonial domains against the introduction of heresy." [3]

There were estimates that a fighting force of as many as 20,000 men might be raised among the Indians, but Pike, now commissioned a Confederate brigadier general, was far more conservative. In November 1861, he reported to Richmond that he could muster four regiments, mostly Cherokee, totalling 3,500 men, with detached companies of Seminole bringing the total to 4,000. The Choctaw offered a regiment, and he considered it possible that still another might be raised among the Creek, for a total of 7,500 if arms were supplied. The wild Comanche and Osage, he said, should be employed only in case of invasion—and, indeed, Pike entertained doubts that the Indians should be used at all in conventional warfare.

3. Annie Heloise Abel, *The American Indian as Slaveholder and Secessionist* (Cleveland: Arthur H. Clark Co., 1915), p. 60.

Arkansas troops had their first taste of battle on August 10, 1861, at Wilson's Creek south of Springfield, Missouri, where they joined with local volunteers under Sterling Price. In this first engagement General Price acknowledged that his own state had not entered the Confederacy by eschewing the gray uniform, wearing a plug hat and frock coat as he rode into battle. The poorly organized Union forces were routed and retreated northward, but the Confederates themselves were so badly equipped and beset by problems of divided command they did not pursue their advantage.

The real test of Confederate mettle came early the following year in what may have been the most significant Civil War engagement west of the Mississippi. Under Maj. Gen. Samuel A. Curtis the Federals had driven into northwest Arkansas while Grant took the main force into Tennessee. The Confederates under Maj. Gen. Earl Van Dorn mounted a drive across Missouri to flank Grant. Battle was joined at Pea Ridge in Benton County. After three days of seesaw fighting, which cost more than 2,500 casualties, the Confederate assault petered out and the dispirited troops fell back south to the Boston Mountains.

Albert Pike's Indians were ordered into battle at Pea Ridge and left behind a confused record in which they were accused both of cowardice and savage atrocities. They were mounted troops, and Pike found it necessary to order them to leave their ponies behind in the heavy woods. Fighting in their own way, they took to the trees in the face of Federal cannon fire, for which they were subjected to much ridicule. And some of the tribesmen scalped a few of the enemy, touching off a furore in the Northern press. Although Col. Stand Watie's Cherokee regiment performed well in covering the Confederate retreat, Van Dorn made it clear that he wanted no more of Indian troops. Pike's reward was a satirical personal attack in the *New York Tribune,* which gave him credit for the actions of "the Aboriginal Corps of Tomahawkers and Scalpers at the Battle of Pea Ridge." [4]

Generals Van Dorn and Price were now ordered to remove their forces east of the Mississippi to meet the threat posed by

---

4. Abel, *The American Indian as Slaveholder,* p. 322.

Grant. The Arkansas leaders, with reason, saw this as a move to
write off their state, leaving it virtually undefended against the
Union forces in Missouri and Kansas, and those advancing
south along the Mississippi. The Arkansas delegation to the
Confederate Congress protested vehemently, and Governor Rector went so far as to suggest that the states west of the Mississippi ought to secede from the Confederacy. From now on the
war in Arkansas would be largely a holding operation, with the
Union forces ultimately occupying the principal towns while the
Confederates continued to control most of the southwest section
of the state.

In the hill country irregular forces, called Jayhawkers when
they professed Union allegiance, and Bushwhackers when they
ostensibly fought on the Confederate side, preyed on Arkansans
of all persuasions. Under these circumstances Brig. Gen. William L. Cabell, an Arkansan West Point graduate, was not
registering a complaint but recognizing the logic of the situation
when he reported 1,250 desertions from his command of 3,000
while falling back on Arkadelphia in early 1863. He explained
that "both officers and men were impressed with the idea that
the proper way to defend the country was for each man to go
home and defend his own home." [5]

Military operations in Arkansas began under a state board
chaired by Governor Rector. Motivated by his well-founded
suspicion that the Confederate high command might strip the
state of its defenses, Rector resisted the transfer of authority to
Richmond. The shift of Van Dorn's army east of the Mississippi
opened the way for General Curtis's Union troops to move
south toward Little Rock, while a column under Brig. Gen.
Frederick Steele moved in from southeast Missouri to capture
Batesville en route to Helena, a key point on the Mississippi.
Rector, ignoring the Confederate chain of command, on May 5
issued a call for volunteers for state service and ordered Brig.
Gen. John Selden Roane, a former governor, to take command
of the defense of Arkansas; shipment of recruits to Van Dorn

5. David Y. Thomas, *Arkansas in War and Reconstruction* (Little Rock: United
Daughters of the Confederacy, 1926), p. 199.

was suspended and Texas regiments en route to his army were halted at Pine Bluff and impressed into service. As it turned out, the threatened envelopment of the capital was postponed for more than a year as Curtis, first delayed by floods, also suffered a loss of priority, with most of his Union infantry shifted east of the Mississippi.

Under pressure, Richmond agreed to reconstitute a major command in Arkansas, and assigned to it a Confederate general who was to earn more personal opprobrium from his fellow citizens than any of the Yankees who came as conquerors. Maj. Gen. Thomas C. Hindman, the former congressman from Helena, had earned his spurs fighting with Beauregard in Tennessee. En route to take over what was to become the new Trans-Mississippi Department, he found Memphis falling to the advancing federal armies and recognized that this meant he would have to raise means internally to defend Arkansas. He began by abolishing Rector's state army, conscripting its troops, and impressing its stores. He then launched a conscription drive of his own, paying little attention to legal exemptions prescribed by the Confederate government; those who weren't able to perform regular military service were organized into guerrilla Home Guard units. He ordered up regiments from Texas, stripped Albert Pike's Indian Territory command of its white units and best equipment, established depositories for the storage of cotton that might fall to the advancing enemy, and invoked a Confederate law that allowed him to burn a considerable amount he believed bound to be lost. By June 30 he had extended martial law to cover the whole of his military command, and any who resisted his draconian measures were put under arrest as traitors.

Before the complaints against Hindman reached the point where Richmond was forced to replace him, the hard-handed general did in fact organize Arkansas to defend itself, and he probably deserves primary credit for the fact that the state was able to avoid total subjection during the last two years of the war. On August 12, 1862, Maj. Gen. Theophilus Hunter Holmes took over the department, relegating Hindman to a field command. Among the matters the more temperate new commander tidied up was a raging controversy between Hindman and Albert Pike, in which each preferred court-martial charges against the other—with Pike finally bringing charges against Holmes as well. Pike ultimately left the service and sat out the rest of the war, but he left behind a publicly circulated letter in which he warned Holmes of a "universal malediction that will fall like a great wave of God's just anger on you and the murderous miscreant by whose malign promptings you are making yourself accursed." [6]

In October an election called under a technicality in the constitution adopted by the secession convention ended the tenure of Henry Rector, and replaced him with Harris Flanagin of Clark County, called back from service in Tennessee and Kentucky as colonel of the Second Arkansas Mounted Rifles. The civil government, forced into exile at Washington in Hempstead County after General Steele occupied the capital in September 1863, was left in the shadows by the course of military events. These were stirring enough, a compound of the gallantry, stupidity, courage, and personal pretensions that marked the last of the wars Americans consider romantic.

In December 1862, General Hindman made one more try at invading Missouri, but was turned back at Prairie Grove near Fayetteville. A month later the fort that bore his name at Arkansas Post fell before a combined Union operation that represented one of the great mismatches of the war. Maj. Gen. John A. McLernand, with a force of some 30,000 men and a flotilla of armed riverboats, quickly reduced the isolated log bastion manned by five thousand Confederates under Brig. Gen. Thomas J. Churchill, capturing the entire garrison.

A primary mission of the Trans-Mississippi command was to relieve pressure on the Confederate forces trying to hold off Grant in Tennessee and Mississippi. To that end, on July 4, 1863, Generals Holmes and Price moved against Helena with a force of nearly 8,000 men. The attack was badly planned and dogged by failure of communications; wave after wave assaulted the steep slopes of Crowley's Ridge, to find that when they seized the heights they came under direct fire from entrenched batteries and the guns of naval vessels lying off the

6. Annie Heloise Abel, *The American Indian as Participants in the Civil War* (Cleveland: Arthur H. Clark Co., 1915), p. 351.

Helena waterfront. The four thousand Union defenders lost 57 killed and 146 wounded before the Confederates fell back, but Holmes's casualties ran to 21 percent of his command—to which may be added Brig. Gen. Marsh Walker, who thought his courage and competence were questioned after the battle by Brig. Gen. John S. Marmaduke. That quarrel reached its climax weeks later as the troops under Sterling Price were preparing to abandon Little Rock to General Steele's advancing Yankees, and these two senior officers took time out to fight a duel fatal to Walker.

In fact, the mission at Helena had been aborted before it began; while Arkansas and Missouri men were storming the heights above the river town, Vicksburg was falling to Grant, and far to the northeast Robert E. Lee's daring invasion of Yankee territory was ending in catastrophe at Gettysburg. For all practical purposes the Confederacy was finished on that July Fourth, but there were battles still to be fought. Dashing cavalrymen under Jo Shelby and Marmaduke left legends behind them. Raiding along the banks of the Mississippi, Marmaduke captured two steamers, disabled five gunboats, and damaged five transports moving troops to join Sherman—only to be greeted by complaints from local planters that they had assurances from General Price that they would not be disturbed in their cotton trade. Fine, Marmaduke replied, you gentlemen go on about your business and I'll go on about mine—which is sinking Yankee shipping.

In the spring of 1864 General Steele combined the forces at Fort Smith and Little Rock for a move south to join Gen. Nathaniel P. Banks, who had launched an expedition up the Red River intended to reduce the Trans-Mississippi headquarters at Shreveport and open the way for final conquest of the Southwest. Banks's drive in Louisiana was stalled, and the Arkansas Confederate command claimed a famous victory when Steele was defeated in a series of bloody encounters that forced him to abandon Camden and fall back to Little Rock. But by fall Governor Flanagin was urgently protesting the call from Richmond for still more troops from Arkansas, this time to join the last-ditch effort to halt Sherman's march into Georgia.

Gen. Edmund Kirby Smith, who "ruled the vast region west

of the Mississippi almost as a Persian satrap, so that his department was humorously called 'Kirby-Smithdom,' " concluded that the best way to justify keeping his command intact was to make one last major effort to the north. This brought forth a bitter protest from the Confederate commander in Louisiana, Gen. Richard Taylor: "The substance of Louisiana and Texas was staked against the shadow of Missouri and northern Arkansas." [7]

In late August 12,000 mounted men under Sterling Price headed north across Arkansas, accompanied by Thomas C. Reynolds, Missouri's governor in exile, who expected to be installed in the statehouse at Jefferson City. General Price always contended that this extraordinary cavalry sweep of almost fifteen hundred miles was worthwhile, claiming that he captured and paroled 3,000 prisoners, while inflicting property damage running to $10 million, and he insisted that he was so warmly welcomed by Missouri's German settlers he had every reason to believe that he could have raised an army of 50,000 men had he been able to stay through the winter. Price's thrust reached as far as Independence on the Kansas border, but the ad hoc army melted away in the long retreat down the Missouri–Kansas–Arkansas line to Texas.

By late 1864 Federal forces occupied Little Rock, Helena, Pine Bluff, DeValls Bluff, Fort Smith, Van Buren, and Fayetteville—but no one controlled the countryside. Jo Shelby, ranging up the White River Valley, reported the area at the mercy of roving bands of armed men: "Confederate soldiers in nothing save the name, robbers, and jayhawkers have vied with Federals in plundering, devouring and wasting the substance of loyal Southerners." He found these intruders "sweltering in the hot fumes of Memphis whiskey," and contemptuously impressed them into his own force under threat of hanging.[8] Down in Chicot County, John MacLean wrote to Gen. D. H. Reynolds: "One thing I do believe, that we are a very great distance from the Confederacy and the Federacy, in fact it

---

7. Clement Eaton, *A History of the Southern Confederacy* (New York: Free Press, 1965), p. 202.

8. Thomas, *Arkansas in War and Reconstruction,* p. 274.

seems like we are a considerable distance from anywhere."[9]

Kirby Smith, who considered himself the ordained inheritor of the collapsing Confederate government, sent emissaries to inquire if Emperor Maximilian of Mexico might be interested in backing a Confederate redoubt in the Southwest, and an approach was made in his name to Napoleon III, who was offered emancipation of the slaves as the price of French support. The *Washington Telegraph,* the last newspaper in Arkansas to escape Federal control, supported these wistful efforts, calling for abandonment of "all pretense and hollow forms of self-government" in return for alliance with any available crowned head.[10]

The war was over in Arkansas. Nothing remained but the stacking of arms as Confederate units worked out surrender arrangements with local Union commanders. Governor Flanagin offered to negotiate on behalf of the Confederate state government, but when the authorities at Little Rock did not choose to recognize him, he simply delivered the archives and went home to Arkadelphia. Isaac Murphy, the lone dissenter at the secession convention, was sitting as unionist governor, and in May he proclaimed an end to hostilities.

9. George H. Thompson, *Arkansas and Reconstruction* (Port Washington, N.Y.: Kennikat Press, 1976), p. 36.

10. Thomas, *Arkansas in War and Reconstruction,* p. 308.

9

Reconstruction

*T*HE burdens of war did not fall equally upon Arkansans. Those in the northwestern section of the state, who had been most reluctant to sunder the Republic, suffered the greatest damage from the collision of Union and Confederate armies, and from the depredations of the Jayhawkers and Bushwhackers who ranged the hill country. In 1865 Gov. Isaac Murphy reported widespread destitution and suffering in the area, and the Arkansas historian David Y. Thomas thought it probably worse than that in any southern state—yet he found that the plantation country south of the Arkansas River had been largely immune to such marauding.

In the towns where the occupying troops exercised actual control there seems to have been little real oppression. Thomas's history, published by the United Daughters of the Confederacy, paid this tribute to the senior Yankee commander: "General Frederick Steele proved to be a kind and conciliatory enemy and, instead of seeking to crush [the Confederates] with his heel, sought to bring them back to the flag they once loved. The names of some Union commanders may be anathema in Arkansas, but that of Steele is not." The citizens of Little Rock left his name on one of their grade schools—this despite the fact that he ordered the hanging of an authentic hero, seventeen-year-old David O. Dodd, who earned a place in the South's pantheon by refusing to identify the source of reports he tried to smuggle through the lines, saying: "I will not betray a friend, and, like Nathan Hale, my only regret is that I have but one life to give for my country." [1]

With Steele's occupation of the capital, in September 1863, political action was again possible for Arkansans willing to take an oath of loyalty to the federal government. Those whose prewar designation had been Unionist or Unconditional Unionist now became known as Radical Unionist or Radical Republican; the opposition was simply labeled "Conservative." When the *Arkansas Gazette* received a proposal that the newspaper continue publication in support of the new military regime, the majority partner, C. C. Danley, refused to take the oath on the ground that he would make a better federal prisoner than federal editor. The occupation forces took over the newspaper plant, and by January there issued from it the *Unconditional Union,* edited by William Meade Fishback, a Fort Smith lawyer who refugeed to Saint Louis and returned to Arkansas with Steele's army.

On December 8, Lincoln issued an amnesty proclamation, providing that Arkansas could establish a civilian administration by election when 10 percent of the total of voters registered in 1860 had taken the loyalty oath. The Radicals pushed ahead with organization of the state government under a constitution drafted at a dubious convention made up of delegates purporting to represent twenty-four counties. The 1836 constitution was modified to provide immediate emancipation of the slaves, and a provisional government was established under Isaac Murphy to serve pending a ratifying election on March 14. Washington accepted the arrangement, and a drive began to qualify by oath the 5,406 electors required for validation. There was considerable leverage available in the Confiscation Act, which classified rebel-owned property as abandoned and required that it could be made available only to those willing to affirm their loyalty. The threatened loss of valuable holdings brought the reluctant Danley and other leading citizens into the Federal fold, nominally at least.

The March election ratified the new constitution by a vote of

1. David Y. Thomas, *Arkansas in War and Reconstruction* (Little Rock: United Daughters of the Confederacy, 1926), pp. 221, 150.

12,177 to 226, confirmed Murphy as governor, and named three congressmen; in April the new legislature elected Fishback and Elisha Baxter to the Senate, but Congress refused to seat the Arkansas delegation and the state remained in limbo. It also turned out that Isaac Murphy was as frugal as he was stubborn, and by November the more rapacious members of the legislature were in rebellion against his austere fiscal policies.

Arkansas finished out the war under this demigovernment, the product of President Lincoln's doomed effort to ease the rebellious states back into the Union with minimum retribution. In April 1865, a special session of the legislature unanimously ratified the Thirteenth Amendment abolishing slavery. This action presaged the subsequent demand for full citizenship, which would bring into focus the critical matter of suffrage, around which politics in Arkansas revolved for the next decade. At issue was not only the federal government's enfranchisement of the freedmen, but the demand of Radical Republicans that ex-Confederate soldiers and their active political supporters be disfranchised. This was the double-edged issue that set a militant Congress against Lincoln and his successor, Andrew Johnson.

In the period called Presidential Reconstruction, 1865–1867, the Conservatives gained control of the Arkansas legislature after a state supreme court ruling in 1866 effectively invalidated the anti-Confederate provision of the voting oath. Governor Murphy had the state government working again in reasonably good order and insofar as he could he generally tempered the policies sent down from Washington. But even if he had been disposed to, he could hardly have stood in the way of the federal demand that the freed blacks must be admitted to full citizenship. Yet the Arkansas legislature, disregarding its precarious situation, refused to ratify the Fourteenth Amendment with its guarantee of equal protection under the law, instead enacting statutes arbitrarily regulating the labor of blacks and denying them the right to sit on juries, serve in the militia, or attend white public schools.

The Conservative majority elected two prominent and presumably unrepentant Confederates to the United States Senate, voted financial aid for Confederate veterans, and seriously considered a vote of thanks to the imprisoned Jefferson Davis for his services to the Confederacy. These moves, of course, provided prime ammunition for Radical Republicans bent on scuttling the mild Presidential Reconstruction. In March 1867, Congress overrode President Johnson's veto and declared illegal the existing governments in Arkansas and nine other southern states.

Congressional Reconstruction was initiated by relegating former Confederate states to five military districts, of which Arkansas and Mississippi made up the fourth. The district commander, Gen. Edward O. C. Ord, was given plenary powers, including the right to substitute military tribunals for the extant courts. It was stipulated that this regime would continue until the state obtained congressional approval for a new constitution fully guaranteeing the civil rights of blacks, ratified the Fourteenth Amendment, and imposed as a qualification for voting an "ironclad oath" that effectively disfranchised all but "negroes, wartime Unionists, draft dodgers, Southerners too old or too young for military service in the war, and carpetbaggers." [2]

General Ord arrived in Little Rock in the spring of 1867 and, finding that the tight-fisted Murphy had the state government in sound financial shape, allowed the old mountaineer to continue in office. But objectionable laws like the one providing financial aid for ex-Confederates were voided, and the Conservative legislature was not allowed to meet again. The Republican party of Arkansas was formally organized and General Ord turned over to it the task of registering voters.

With the assistance of the new Freedmen's Bureau, and the unofficial but equally active Union League, registration committees by November had signed up 33,047 whites and 21,969 blacks. A minority of the white registrants belonged to the enfeebled Democratic party revived by those who rationalized the oath, privately declaring it coercive and therefore nonbinding. This was the constituency that named seventy-five delegates to the constitutional convention assembled at Little Rock in January 1868. Thomas quotes a contemporary description of the

2. John L. Ferguson and J. H. Atkinson, *Historic Arkansas* (Little Rock: Arkansas History Commission, 1966), p. 148.

election: "Democrats intimidated Negroes, and Republicans stuffed the ballot box at will, voted women and children, and voted 'early and often,' traveling from ballot-box to ballot-box." [3]

There were only nine native Arkansans among those convened to determine the state's future, and three of these were ex-slaves. There were twenty-three carpetbaggers newly arrived to exploit the possibilities of Reconstruction, thirty scalawags, as unionist locals were called, and a dozen of the old Conservatives. The *Gazette,* now publishing daily under the direction of the founder's son, Maj. William E. Woodruff, Jr., late of the Confederate artillery, scorned the constitutional convention:

> The bastard collocation whose putridity stinks in the nostrils of all decency, now in session at the capitol, has very conceited ideas of its importance and pretentious opinions of the scope of its powers. As a matter of some trifling interest to those who have not witnessed the exhibition of the menagerie, we would state that the Negro members, eight in number, occupy seats on the western side of the hall.

This drew a resounding response from the convention's most conspicuous carpetbagger, the bearded, bull-voiced Joseph Brooks, a Methodist minister from Iowa who had arrived in Arkansas as chaplain of a Negro regiment: "We claim the right to be here. They may confront us here and elsewhere with such slang as that which has been employed in regard to the odor of our members and our constituents. I have only to say, sir, that if I am to elect between the two, if I am to choose between the odor of my constituents and the smell of treason, which 'smells to heaven,' then I affiliate over this way to all eternity!" [4]

The leader of the Conservatives, Jesse N. Cypert, a former Confederate major from Searcy who had served in the secession convention, tried to stave off the inevitable by urging that the mild constitution of 1864 be readopted with amendments, but the effort failed. A new charter was shouted through by a vote of forty-five to twenty-two, with the minority refusing to sign.

3. Thomas, *Arkansas in War and Reconstruction,* p. 416.

4. John Gould Fletcher, *Arkansas* (Chapel Hill: University of North Carolina Press, 1947), p. 208.

Cypert gave his sardonic benediction to the raucous proceedings: ''I have had a little experience in revolutionary movements. Six years ago I heard just such a clamor from those galleries as I heard a while ago. It shocked me then—it shocks me now.'' [5]

Joseph Brooks, the bellwether of the constitutional convention, was passed over when the Republicans met to make the nominations that would create a new state government. Leadership was conferred upon a thirty-five-year old ex-cavalryman who would dominate the state's affairs during Congressional Reconstruction, and continue as Republican party leader until his death in 1913. Powell Clayton came to Arkansas in 1862 with a Kansas regiment, distinguished himself in combat, and finished the war as a brigadier general in command of Federal forces in the Pine Bluff area. He elected to stay on, bought a plantation nearby, and married a southern belle whose father had served with General Hindman's Confederate corps.

Inevitably, the new constitution and the Republican ticket carried at the polls in March. The *Gazette* found that the state's principal officers, and seven of the nine circuit judges, had been absolutely unknown to the people of the state sixty days before their election or appointment. In the legislative branch the Radicals had majorities of eighty-two to one in the house, and twenty-one to one in the senate. In Congress Thaddeus Stevens moved to readmit Arkansas to the Union, but with the proviso that the new constitution should never be amended to deny the vote to any citizen now enfranchised under it. President Johnson vetoed the act, Congress overrode, and Arkansas became a state again on June 22, 1868.

Powell Clayton was inaugurated governor on July 2. Forty-five years later he described the occasion in a sententious memoir, recalling that he had turned out in full fig to find that the outgoing governor, Isaac Murphy, wore his accustomed homespun. As the two rode together to the capitol in an open carriage Murphy took note of the general's white gloves and said he thought only dudes wore such trappings in the summertime.

5. Fletcher, *Arkansas,* p. 210.

"Governor," Clayton quoted himself, "it is not the garb that makes the man, yet in deference to your opinion, and especially in view of the character of the work I am about to enter upon today, which will doubtless require 'handling without gloves,' I now remove mine." In the privacy of the executive office the retiring governor offered a characteristic salute to his successor, reaching into a straw-filled barrel to bring forth a stone jug; Clayton duly acknowledged the authority of "the real mountain dew." [6]

Powell Clayton did indeed take off the gloves. In the November election he delivered the state's electoral votes to U. S. Grant by invalidating the registration in twelve heavily Democratic counties, thereby permitting the Republicans to name all three of the state's congressmen. The legislature was in his pocket and provided new taxes and bond issues as a source of patronage for the statehouse machine and its local affiliates; under Radical rule the state's indebtedness of some $3 million increased by $10 million, and the total for the counties, municipalities, and school districts was even larger.

Arkansas cherishes few of the legends of harsh repression that are the heritage of Reconstruction in other Confederate states. But most of Arkansas's new rulers had only recently traded their blue uniforms for civilian clothes, and most assumed, as conquerors always have, that where there are victors there must be spoils. "The 'reconstructors' of [Arkansas] were certainly, in the main, a set of ruthless robbers," Charles Nordhoff of the *New York Herald* wrote after a tour of the state early in 1875. He found government at all levels bankrupt,

and for this huge indebtedness . . . the people have nothing to show. . . . The schools are almost all closed because the school fund was stolen; and Little Rock is unpaved, though the conquerors of 1868 issued nearly enough shinplasters to pave all the streets handsomely with the paper itself, and bonds enough besides to make dry crossings at the corners. . . . All these local appointees of the Central government had unlimited power to steal, and they

6. Margaret Ross, "Chronicles of Arkansas," *Arkansas Gazette,* Sept. 4, 1959.

knew it. Indeed, they were expected to divide their plunder with the ring at headquarters.'' [7]

There were comparable opportunities in the private sector. While the fighting was still in progress cotton became an increasingly valuable commodity, and there were soldiers and civilians who could see the possibilities inherent in the fact that staple seized by the federal authorities and sold in Arkansas for fourteen cents a pound would go for forty to fifty cents if a way could be found to ship it to Saint Louis. After 1863 it became the practice to use "abandoned" plantations in the southeast section of the state as depositories for slave families uprooted by the advance of the Union armies, and these were leased to private operators. John S. Phelps, a political emissary of President Lincoln, reported that a Union general at Helena was "swapping contraband for cotton, two niggers per bale," and acidly observed that this was not considered a violation of the order against returning fugitive slaves, but a legitimate business practice.[8]

An example of uninhibited entrepreneurial talent was provided by Daniel P. Upham, who arrived from New York in the spring of 1865. He had only ten dollars in his pocket, but that meager stake was supplemented by close personal connections to Brig. Gen. Alexander Shaler, in command of the occupation forces in the area around DeValls Bluff. Pooling his influence with cash provided by three new arrivals from Saint Louis, Upham leased two thousand acres of prime cotton land, and put one hundred freed slaves and seventy-five mules to work. At the end of a year his share of the profit was estimated at from $200,000 to $300,000 and he was ready to spread out into the saloon, mercantile, and steamboating trade.

At Little Rock, on a ridge overlooking the Arkansas River, a street was named Lincoln Avenue in honor of the martyred president. Before Reconstruction ended this thoroughfare was lined by handsome Victorian mansions occupied by Governor Clayton and the more successful carpetbaggers. The natives gave the imposing array a name of their own: Robber's Row.

7. Ross, "Chronicles of Arkansas," *Arkansas Gazette,* Nov. 12, 1958.
8. Thomas, *Arkansas in War and Reconstruction,* p. 367.

Powell Clayton had no illusion that Arkansans would take kindly to his regime. By the time of the 1868 general election the Radicals had found, or created, enough disorder to prompt the governor to put ten counties under martial law, and others were added later. Clayton justified his action on the ground that white-robed night riders posed a threat of outright rebellion, although the fact seems to be that their primary mission was to counteract by intimidation the Union League's campaign to herd blacks to the polls by means hardly less reprehensible. Clayton also cited acts of violence against white Radicals, and certainly there were some—although the Conservative leaders steadfastly denied that these could be attributed to organized activity, and refused to concede that the Ku Klux Klan even existed in Arkansas.

Clayton had trouble obtaining arms for his predominately black militia, finally purchasing 4,000 muskets and a supply of ammunition in Saint Louis. This cargo was aboard the steamboat *Hesper* below Memphis when she was boarded in the night by masked men who deposited the arms on the bottom of the Mississippi. Congress largely ignored Clayton's complaint of piracy, but he managed to scrape up 2,000 additional muskets and his militia began to range fourteen counties.

"For a time," David Y. Thomas wrote, "the Ku Klux hunted the militia, and the militia hunted the Ku Klux." [9] Before the state force was disbanded in 1869 there were serious clashes in Sevier, Pope, and Conway counties, and Jayhawking again flourished along the Missouri border. There were spectacular casualties among the politicians on both sides. James Hinds, a leading Radical figure, was killed, and Joseph Brooks was seriously wounded, when they were shot down from ambush while riding to a political rally in Clarendon.

In what is still regarded as the state's most famous unsolved crime the irascible old Confederate, T. C. Hindman, came to a bloody end while sitting quietly in his home at Helena. He had recently engaged in a sulphurous public debate with Powell Clayton, followed a few days later by his arrest on a treason charge, and on the day of his death the populace of the river

9. Thomas, *Arkansas in War and Reconstruction,* p. 421.

town had been inflamed by a posse that hunted down and lynched a black fugitive. The identity of the assassin who stood in the dark on the general's porch was never established, and the victim, possibly recognizing how wide was the range of possibilities, told those who attended him: "I do not know who killed me, but, whoever it was, I forgive him." [10]

Beneath the surface tensions and sporadic outbreaks of violence Arkansans, white and black, were coming to terms with the new, stark necessities of their existence. The Confederacy had collapsed in a welter of inflation which wiped out the value of its currency and bonds, and the heavy investment in slaves was swept away; the economic consequences may be seen in the fact that when civilian government was restored in 1864 the value of real property, set at $153,699,473 in 1860, was assessed at $30,000,000; and the effort to collect taxes on that base brought in only $257.97 in specie and $2,565.80 in warrants. The problem, recognized by all but the most unrealistic of the Radical "reconstructors," was to bring the emancipated blacks and the bankrupt whites together under a system that would restore the agricultural productivity upon which the state depended.

The circumstances produced the solution, and by 1867 advertisements, like this from the *Gazette,* were common: "One hundred laborers wanted to work on a plantation on the Arkansas River. Proprietors to bear all expenses and will pay one-fourth of the crops; or will give number-one hands $240.00 a year with provisions, food, comfortable houses and firewood." [11] Thus sharecropping was born. It would prove a blight to whites and blacks alike in the years to come, and at its worst it properly could be condemned as the replacement of slavery with a form of peonage. But it provided a means of survival for both races in a desperate time, and if anyone had a feasible alternative it was not heard of in Arkansas.

Under this dispensation, as under slavery, the plantation system could not have continued to exist without an effective mea-

10. Thomas, *Arkansas in War and Reconstruction,* p. 341.
11. Fletcher, *Arkansas,* pp. 201, 202.

sure of good will uniting the planter and his hands in their common task. While many blacks drifted away from their home places during the dislocations of the war, a significant number stayed on the land or went south as refugees with their masters. Theirs was a conscious act of loyalty, for with the coming of the occupation forces genuine options opened, and the slaves were exposed to active recruitment with the inducement not only of freedom but of revenge. This continued now, as the Freedmen's Bureau found its charitable and educational programs bent to serve the ends of carpetbag politicians.

When they briefly returned to power the Conservatives enacted measures denying their loyal retainers the most elementary standards of justice. Yet by a remarkable process of rationalization, a considerable majority of both races confined their personal feelings of opprobrium to unprincipled leaders and those they scornfully regarded as their witless dupes—thereby absolving the men and women of different pigmentation with whom they amiably consorted in the conduct of their ordinary affairs. Although there were now agitators aplenty among the freed slaves, and armed black men wearing the late enemy's uniform, there seems to have been remarkably little of the panic fear of black retribution that beset white Arkansans in prewar years.

A sprinkling of blacks attained positions of prominence in Arkansas under Reconstruction. Some were carpetbaggers, educated in the North, coming down to seek their fortunes under the auspices of the Freedmen's Bureau and the Union League. They often gained a surprising acceptance from the white natives, even when they moved into the sensitive area of law enforcement. Mifflin Wister Gibbs, a black Philadelphia lawyer who sat on the municipal bench in Little Rock in 1873, published an autobiography in which he recalled readily establishing a sound and generally amiable working relationship with the white members of the local bar.

William H. Grey, the outstanding black leader of the period, settled at Helena in 1865 after a career as a cook on riverboats operating out of Saint Louis. Born free in the District of Columbia in 1829, the literate and hard-working Grey set up in business as a grocer and baker, but was soon caught up in Reconstruction politics. He was a delegate to the 1868 constitutional convention and a member of the state legislature it created. From 1872 to 1874 he served as commissioner of immigration and state lands, and his political status was attested by his selection to second the nomination of U. S. Grant at the 1872 Republican convention, the first black to address a national party gathering. Grey served in the state senate after Reconstruction and later as Phillips County Clerk.

The *Gazette,* appraising the quality of the black members of the legislature in 1873, conceded that there were among them men of considerable ability and independence as well as poorly educated countrymen clearly being used by their Radical Republican bosses. Rating Rep. W. Hines Furbush of Phillips as "something of a demagogue" the account nevertheless conceded his intelligence and capacity for leadership. The recognized prowess of the legislature's leading champion of civil rights, a black carpetbagger from Ohio, was explained on the ground that he was "one of those who would like to thrust himself into white society." The reporter wrote admiringly of another's ability to spellbind any audience, and asked, "in fact, was there ever a colored man who couldn't?" [12]

Complaints about the corruption and inefficiency of the carpetbag government were intensified by the frustration and resentment of the native politicians who found themselves effectively disfranchised under the new constitution. But contemporary accounts indicate that business, political and otherwise, still managed to go on pretty much as usual. The *Gazette* described the scene in the statehouse: "The old structure is fast going to ruin, and is badly in need of repair throughout. A walk through it will disclose the Arkansas office-holder in all varieties, from the pleasant agreeable gentleman to the cross, angry, suspicious carpetbagger." [13] Without the pejorative identification of the irritable bureaucrat, it is a description that might have applied at almost any period in the state's history.

12. Ross, "Chronicles of Arkansas," *Arkansas Gazette,* Jan. 22, 1967.
13. Ross, "Chronicles of Arkansas," *Arkansas Gazette,* July 10, 1966.

10

The Yankees Go Home

*F*OR almost a decade after the end of the Civil War Arkansas's political leaders were divided tactically on the question of whether to treat the carpetbag government as an illegal usurpation of power—as most whites regarded it—or to take the ironclad loyalty oath with crossed fingers in order to be able to counter the Radical Republicans at the polls. For the conservatives to join direct political battle with Powell Clayton's carpetbag administration was to recognize it as the *de facto* government of the state, as it indisputably was. But this also implied *de jure* recognition, and thereby weakened the moral argument of the oppressed majority in its appeals to the national leadership in Washington.

David Walker epitomized those who held to the *de jure* position. A Whig leader in northwest Arkansas before the war, Walker had served in the legislature and as a supreme court justice. In 1860 he came as a Union man to the secession convention, where he was elected presiding officer; he departed as an unconvinced member of the majority that voted to take the state out of the Union. It was apparently his intention to sit out the war, but after Federal forces had seized his extensive property at Fayetteville he entered the Confederate army in 1863 as a colonel of cavalry and a military judge. Shortly thereafter he wrote in his journal a remarkably prescient justification for his change of heart:

Whatever may have been the policy of the Federal Government at the outset, there can *now* be no doubt but that its fixed and settled purpose is to free the negroes and settle them permanently in the slaveholding states, to assert and maintain for them equal legal and political rights with the white population. To secure this end, they will appoint civil officers to administer the laws, until the negro and abolition vote is sufficiently strong to elect to office their representative men. Most of the prominent Southern men would at once be arrested and imprisoned, after which a proclamation would likely be issued pardoning all such as give in their allegiance to the old government. Stringent laws touching treason and rebellion will be passed.[1]

Although he did not wind up in prison at the conclusion of the war, Walker found it necessary to obtain a presidential pardon before he could reclaim his property. This was granted at the behest of his former unionist compatriot, Gov. Isaac Murphy, who urged him to join in working for internal unity, suggesting that so far as possible he ignore the bloody-shirt rhetoric emanating from Washington: "Our position there depends upon our behavior *here*—if we establish justice at home we can demand it with good face abroad. If we secure to all the good citizens of the state equal rights—the state is sure to obtain her just rights." [2] Walker appears to have acted upon this advice, for he was elected chief justice of the state supreme court during the brief period of Presidential Reconstruction.

In 1866 he wrote the unanimous opinion in *Hawkins* vs. *Filkin* which embodied the *de jure* view of postwar governance Walker never abandoned. The case involved the effort of the defendant to invalidate a promissory note on the ground that the Confederate court which had upheld the claim against him had no legal existence. At issue, of course, was the validity of all the legal actions undertaken under the Confederate regime, and Walker's constitutional argument derived from the states' rights doctrine that was to be the mainstay of the beleaguered South:

1. George H. Thompson, *Arkansas and Reconstruction* (Port Washington, N.Y.: Kennikat Press, 1976), pp. 52, 53.
2. Thompson, *Arkansas and Reconstruction,* p. 55.

> [I]n the Civil War just closed, there was but one great political question at issue, which was as to the power of the state to dissolve its connection with the national government—in which, by a conflict of arms, it has been settled that such power does not exist. That is the question, and the only question settled. In all other respects the compact remains just as it was previous to the war, and this change is but a change in the construction of a compact. The powers of the two governments, state and federal, remain the same—the rights of the people the same.[3]

With the advent of Congressional Reconstruction Walker withdrew from the government and from direct political involvement. He refused to take the ironclad loyalty oath, and he urged other Conservative leaders to abstrain from participation in elections called under arrangements imposed by the military authorities, and later by the Clayton regime. To vote, he contended, was to accept the legitimacy of the 1868 constitution, whereas a widespread boycott by Conservative white voters would dramatize the fact that the *de facto* government was supported only by a minority made up of blacks, scalawags, and carpetbaggers.

Men of equal stature and probity took the opposite tack, among them Augustus Garland, an ex-Whig who had served in the Confederate Congress and now joined the Conservative leaders who formed the Democratic Central Committee. This group concluded that internal divisions within the Republican regime provided an opportunity for coalition politics that might gain the most immediate objective, repeal of the restrictive loyalty oath. By 1869 the *Gazette,* voicing committee policy, was urging all loyal Democrats to take the oath so they could register and vote.

Walker continued to demur, and he passed on through Garland his stringent criticism of what he regarded as the *Gazette's* immoderate efforts to *"whip in* all who hesitated to follow," a tactic that reminded him of the effort of the secessionists to insure unity for their cause. William E. Woodruff, Jr., in a letter to Walker, conceded that the Democrats had abandoned principle for the time being, but contended that any means were jus-

---

3. Thompson, *Arkansas and Reconstruction,* p. 59.

tified in the necessary effort "to destroy the enemy." The editor argued that there was no "binding force in law or morals to an oath taken under duress," and pursued his military analogy to the point of insisting that in thus practicing and preaching calculated duplicity he no more endangered his immortal soul than he had when he killed Yankees in battle.[4]

Walker's reply bluntly raised a publicly unspoken ethical consideration that has dogged Arkansas politicians from that day to this:

> I have believed and yet believe that we should have adhered to that plank in the Democratic platform which treats the Reconstruction Acts, and the State Governments made under them, as void. But it seems we are to abandon this plank, and step off squarely on the negro equality plank of the Radical platform and urge its adoption, to swear never to abandon it, and to invite the negroes to get upon it and vote with us. Are you in earnest in all this? Do you realy (*sic*) intend to fasten negro suffrage and negro equality upon the State? If such is realy (*sic*) your intention, then I can see how in good faith the voters oath may be taken, but if it is intended that this position shall be assumed, and the negro vote used to enable us to get in power that we may disfranchise him—Then, then—no, I will give no utterance to my feelings.[5]

Here, recast by the outcome of the lost war, was the unresolved moral dilemma that had faced Arkansas's antebellum leaders as they grappled with the issue of slavery. As a class, these conservative men were not less concerned with human justice than their contemporaries elsewhere in the Union, but they were in a situation in which the enforced application of egalitarian principle would have disruptive practical consequences. As would be the case with many of their successors in the century to come, the positions they took on racial matters were almost entirely devoid of ideological roots; white supremacy would later become a corrupting political slogan, but in that transitional period it was an inescapable social and economic fact of life that could only be altered by the passage of time. No ideal solution was available to them through the political pro-

4. Thompson, *Arkansas and Reconstruction,* p. 85.
5. Thompson, *Arkansas and Reconstruction,* p. 86.

cess, and they had exhausted the possibilities of armed conflict.

Most of the state's leaders went along with the Democratic Central Committee's decision to accord *de jure* recognition to the *de facto* government, swallowing their distaste for the hypocrisy implicit in taking an oath of loyalty to a regime they believed to be constitutionally illegitimate. George H. Thompson in *Arkansas and Reconstruction* traced in detail the developing differences between the two prewar Whig unionists, Garland and Walker, and concluded: "Their behavior seems to have been determined more by personality and character than by political affiliation." [6]

The same judgment probably could be rendered in the case of Powell Clayton. He accepted the Republican party as a necessary instrument of governance and supported the social reforms called for by Reconstruction policy. Faced as he was by the deeply personal opposition of a majority of the native whites he was presumed to govern, he had no option except to function in the manner that apparently came naturally to him—as an unabashed power politician.

There was never any doubt that Clayton considered his own and the party's interests to be identical, nor was there anything obscure about his announced motto: "The men who do the work shall have the rewards." [7] As Augustus Garland anticipated, this kind of heavy-handed administration was bound to produce rifts among the political opportunists who had helped the ex-cavalryman assemble the Republican machine.

The scalawag faction, whose leader, James M. Johnson of Madison County, had to settle for lieutenant governor, resented the dominance of Powell Clayton's carpetbaggers. In 1869 Johnson's followers joined the passed-over Joseph Brooks in an open break with the Radicals, forming the Liberal Republican party with an overt appeal to Democrats and prewar Whigs through a promise to restore the franchise to ex-Confederates. Clayton was now holding onto his office by main strength; he headed off an effort by the rebellious lieutenant governor to

6. Thompson, *Arkansas and Reconstruction,* p. 244.

7. Thompson, *Arkansas and Reconstruction,* pp. 79–80.

seize power while he was out of the state, and after 1870 he faced an impeachment threat from a house of representatives controlled by Liberal Republicans and Democrats.

In 1871 the general assembly elected Clayton to the Senate, but he prudently refused to yield his power base until he could find a way to bar Johnson as his successor. A compromise was worked out whereby Clayton accepted the Senate seat, Johnson settled for secretary of state, and a Clayton henchman, Ozra A. Hadley, became governor. In the election of 1872 the infighting went public; within Republican ranks Clayton's faction, called "Minstrels" because one of the party leaders had once been an end man, faced the "Brindletails," so designated because Brooks's platform manner reminded an observer of an obstreperous brindle bull he had once known. The Brindletails put up a Reform Republican ticket headed by Brooks.

The Democrats declared against the Minstrel slate, but made no gubernatorial nomination of their own. Clayton responded by bringing forth a moderate candidate with appeal for both conservatives and scalawags, the reputable Elisha Baxter of Batesville, who had supported the Union but had refused a colonel's commission because he would not lead troops against his neighbors. Clayton then matched Brooks's pledge to restore voting rights to all citizens. Fraud was widespread on both sides in the November election, but Clayton's men controlled the election machinery and the official returns gave Baxter a margin of 41,000 to 38,000. The rest of the Minstrel slate was declared elected, and the state's electoral votes went to U. S. Grant—although the returns were so questionable Congress later refused to certify them.

Failing to overturn the result in the courts or the legislature, the outraged Brindletails appealed to the Democrats to join in an effort to install Brooks by force. But the alliance had always been an uneasy one and it fell apart as Baxter, with Clayton's approval, moved to submit a constitutional amendment restoring full suffrage to all ex-Confederates. The new governor followed up with nonpartisan appointments, opposed some of the more obviously corrupt Republican legislation, and transferred the public printing from the Radical *Daily Republican* to the Democratic *Arkansas Gazette*. Finally, when the re-enfranchised

Democrats took control of the general assembly in 1873, Baxter supported their proposal for a convention to draw up a new constitution.

Baxter's independence had ended the Radical machine's control of the governor's office, and Clayton now reversed himself and joined Brooks in a last, desperate effort to recover that fountainhead of patronage. The pretext was a Pulaski circuit court ruling on April 15, 1874, declaring that Brooks had been elected governor back in 1872. Key Republican leaders rallied to support the coup. "Poker Jack" McClure, chief justice of the carpetbag state supreme court, administered the oath of office to Brooks, and a militia general, Robert F. Catterson, used his troops to remove Elisha Baxter physically from the statehouse. Brooks called on Washington for support, including arms to enforce his claim to the governorship, and received assurances from Clayton that such would be forthcoming.

Baxter established headquarters at the Anthony House, three blocks down the street from the statehouse, where Brooks had emplaced his militia on the broad lawn. The Democratic leaders lined up to announce their support for Baxter, and the Pulaski County Bar offered its unanimous, if wholly unbinding, opinion that the circuit court ruling was void. Baxter declared martial law, appointing the Confederate colonel, Robert C. Newton, to take command of the militia. His appeal for support to President Grant apparently offset that of Brooks; the federal response was limited to an order to the garrison at the Little Rock Arsenal to station troops between the two factions with orders to fire only if fired upon.

This extraordinary deployment of political and military forces continued for a month and is usually designated in the annals of Arkansas, with more than a touch of irony, as the Brooks-Baxter War. It was hardly that, but, with all its musical comedy aspects, it was an encounter of profound significance.

The Brooks "army" at the time of the occupation consisted of about three hundred black militiamen under white command. H. King White, a Pine Bluff planter who had ridden with Morgan's Raiders in Kentucky, offered to raise a similar force. Baxter accepted, and White returned on the steamboat *Mary*

Boyd with a cargo of three hundred black field hands, the mayor of Pine Bluff, leading citizens, and a brass band. The liberators marched to the Anthony House singing:

> *Do you see that boat come around the bend?*
> *Goodbye, my lover, goodbye;*
> *It's loaded down with Baxter men,*
> *Goodbye, my lover, goodbye!* [8]

The "Baxter Song" would sound frequently in the days to come as armed patrols from the two forces wandered around the downtown streets where the stores, and most notably the saloons, remained open. The federal troops provided an effective barrier until the very end, when the combatants had grown to about two thousand on each side. There was even putative artillery support. The Brooks forces brought in two field pieces from Fayetteville, and the Baxterites dug up and unspiked an abandoned sixty-four-pound Confederate seige gun, Lady Baxter, which still stands in a place of honor in front of the Old Statehouse in Little Rock. Major Woodruff brought in two cannon from Galveston and these were duly garlanded with flowers by admiring ladies when they were moved into position near the Anthony House.

Governor Baxter spent a good deal of his time and energy restraining his hot-blooded supporters during the month-long confrontation, and it appears that Brooks was no more anxious for a military showdown. Even so there were scattered skirmishes, including one river engagement at Palarm Creek above Little Rock where Baxter men aboard the *Hallie* attempted to intercept a flatboat full of arms coming down from Fayetteville. King White managed to work up a brief battle south of Pine Bluff. At the end of the "war" the *Gazette* estimated the casualties at twenty dead and forty wounded; *Historic Arkansas* reckoned the total dead at two hundred, but conceded that most of the fatalities were accidental, a designation that presumably could cover victims of barroom brawls.

While the troops postured in the streets of Little Rock, the

8. John Gould Fletcher, *Arkansas* (Chapel Hill: University of North Carolina Press, 1947), p. 241.

political maneuvering was centered in Washington. The distinguished Little Rock attorney, U. M. Rose, went to the capital to argue the case for Baxter, and Powell Clayton pleaded with the administration on Brooks's behalf. On April 22 President Grant cautiously endorsed Baxter's proposal that the dispute be submitted to the legislature. Brooks insisted that the matter should go to the state supreme court, which did in fact uphold his claim after two of the carpetbag judges were apparently kidnapped, only to turn up unharmed two days later.

President Grant's patience ran out on May 15. He issued a proclamation recognizing the legislature's designation of Elisha Baxter as the rightful governor, and ordered the Brooks forces to disperse. In July a constitutional convention met, with only four black delegates among the Republican minority. The new constitution restored the franchise to all whites, but also guaranteed full civil rights for the ex-slaves, and many black voters were in the three-to-one majority that ratified the charter in a special election in October.

Elisha Baxter, offered the chance to continue as governor, replied with perhaps the most unusual message ever to issue from that office: "Under the peculiar circumstances which exist, I deem it better and more honorable to decline a nomination dictated, in some measure, by a feeling of gratitude." [9] His replacement was Augustus H. Garland, who had emerged as a prototype of the Bourbon "redeemers" then arising within the reborn Democratic party to restore native rule across the South. The demise of Radical Reconstruction in Arkansas was certified early in 1875 when a special congressional investigating committee returned to Washington from Little Rock to recommend that the Garland administration be allowed to stand.

The swirling political currents that brought on the Brooks-Baxter War produced some splendid ironies. In the late war the unionist Elisha Baxter had been taken prisoner by Colonel Newton, who now organized his militia; King White, who led Baxter's field forces, was a turncoat Clayton supporter; and Brooks put his troops under the command of the doughty Confederate

9. Thompson, *Arkansas and Reconstruction,* p. 163.

brigadier, James F. Fagan. Finally, blacks provided the rank and file on both sides of the engagement that marked the end of Reconstruction in Arkansas. The Brooks-Baxter War provided a fittingly bizarre climax for an outrageous era.

11

Of Land and Credit

"CREDIT supports agriculture, as the rope supports the hanged," Louis XIV once observed.[1] The aphorism was to apply with particular force in the area the French king originally claimed in Arkansas; from the time of John Law's Mississippi Bubble those who sought their fortune in the land-rich, capital-poor territory were dependent upon a line of credit, and it formed a noose for many.

When the general assembly met for the first time under the statehood constitution of 1836 it recognized as the initial order of business the effort to find a means of converting the potential value of newly cleared acreage into operating funds. Pledging the faith and credit of the state, the legislature created two central banks: the Arkansas State Bank, with three branches, was the fiduciary agent of the government; the Real Estate Bank, with four branches, was created expressly to promote the plantation system. In a panic-ridden era which saw the collapse of institutions that drew resources and management from long-established eastern financial centers there was little chance that the ambitious amateur bankers at Little Rock could buck the tide. By 1839 the currency issued by the State Bank had depreciated to thirty cents on the dollar.

The malfunctioning of the Real Estate Bank left an even

---

1. Sidney Baldwin, *Poverty and Politics* (Chapel Hill: University of North Carolina Press, 1968), p. 42.

deeper imprint on the state's political consciousness. This was actually a private institution controlled by 284 stockholders described as "an economic aristocracy . . . to a large degree an extension of political aristocracy" employing the state's bonding power to create a "system of economic privilege." [2] The plantation belt proprietors undermined the shaky structure when they issued $500,000 in bonds to secure a loan of $250,000—of which they actually received less than $122,000 from the New York bank which sold the bonds to a London financier, James Holford, for $325,000.

In 1840 Archibald Yell made the banking system an issue in his campaign for governor, and upon election launched an investigation that turned up evidence of fraud as well as mismanagement. By 1844 both bank systems were closed, bringing on financial ruin for thousands of individuals, and leaving the state government saddled with debts of more than $3 million. The political issues arising from default on what came to be called the Holford bonds were to haunt every state administration until the end of the century.

Governor Yell took the position that his obligation to preserve the state's faith and credit did not require that he recognize as a just debt state bonds fraudulently issued and illegally disposed of. Supporting Yell, the *Gazette* injected the class issue: "That we should be taxed to pay the debts of the most aristocratic monopoly of land holders in the United States is unbearable." [3]

So the state withdrew from the banking business, and in 1846 an amendment to the constitution provided that no lending institution of any kind could be incorporated in Arkansas, a proscription that prevailed until after the Civil War. The result was to create a system of credit provided by the suppliers and brokers with whom the planters and lesser farmers dealt, adding a heavy override to the cost of borrowed money. Initially the planters were dependent upon New Orleans factors who sold their cotton and shipped them necessary supplies; in the late forties their counterparts began to appear in the Arkansas ports.

2. George H. Thompson, *Arkansas and Reconstruction* (Port Washington, N.Y.: Kennikat Press, 1976), p. 179.

3. Thompson, *Arkansas and Reconstruction,* p. 180.

This operation was hardly adapted to fostering the growth of family farms carved out of the forests beyond the river bottoms. The capital that came into the state for investment or loan in the antebellum period was channeled primarily to the few land-owners whose holdings could be adapted to large-scale production of cotton with slave labor.

The kind of self-serving mismanagement that characterized the state's venture into banking was duplicated in the disposition of lands made available by the federal government to finance public improvements. Fourteen million acres were thus disposed of by 1858 in transactions typified by the record for 1841, when 500,000 acres were sold at a minimum price of two dollars per acre, while returning a net yield to the state of less than a dollar. When 8,600,000 acres of swamp and overflowed land were used as the basis for $2,500,000 in state script to pay for flood control work on the Arkansas and Mississippi rivers, most of the earthworks built by local levee districts were so mislocated or poorly constructed they were swept away in the floods of 1858 and 1859.

By the 1850s railroad fever was running high, and public land grants were used as underwriting for out-of-state promoters who rushed in to form construction companies. The federal government in 1853 authorized the allocation of six sections of land on either side of the right-of-way of the proposed Cairo & Fulton Railroad, with alternate sections assigned to the company and to the state. This line was to traverse Arkansas from the northeast corner, following the old southwesterly military route to Texas, with branches from Little Rock to Fort Smith and Memphis. Although it was not to be completed until after the Civil War, the successor railroad that followed the route, the Saint Louis, Iron Mountain & Southern, became the state's primary transportation system, reversing the flow of commerce downstream to New Orleans, bringing Arkansas into the financial orbit of Saint Louis and Memphis.

Resumption of railroad construction at the end of the Civil War had first priority with the Reconstructors, and this made Powell Clayton heir to the residue left by the aborted state banks, $3,363,509.19 in more-or-less repudiated bonds that had to be cleared away before the state government could go back into the national money markets. Clayton put through legislation necessary to redeem the state's credit, and by the end of 1871 additional bonded indebtedness for railroad construction stood at $6,000,000—for which Arkansas got only 271 miles of railroad, although the carpetbag government had chartered no less than eighty-six railroad companies.

The boodling of state officials, combined with the peculation of outside railroad promoters, kept the operating and construction companies strapped for funds and besieged by creditors. Asa P. Robinson, the able engineer who finally completed the Little Rock & Fort Smith branch line, wrote his principals in Boston regarding the possibility of receivership as a means of discounting outstanding debts, including interest on state bonds:

> It would be a great success if we could get such a receiver as we want, but you see the chance—As matters are situated now we are completely at the mercy of our opponents for Law is the last thing considered in their movements. There never was in the annals of History a more perfect reign of judicial tyranny rascality and lawlessness than now prevails in this state—Numerical strength & force is all that can resist it or else money.[4]

George H. Thompson, examining the record of the Little Rock & Fort Smith, concluded that Powell Clayton acted more responsibly in protecting the public interest than did the railroad promoters in looking after their corporation's securities. In any case the result was disastrous for Arkansas's newly refurbished credit rating; by 1873 potential investors were being assured that they could earn 20 percent interest on a hundred-dollar Arkansas bond purchased for thirty dollars. The decline thereafter was precipitous; by 1879 the same hundred-dollar bond could be had for seven dollars. The average price of Arkansas securities during the period was nineteen, the lowest recorded for twenty-five states.

When the Conservatives came to power in 1874 they rejected the principles and practices of the Radical regime, adopting a constitution that severely limited the taxing and spending pow-

4. Thompson, *Arkansas and Reconstruction*, p. 217.

ers of the state government, and its authority to regulate private business. Fiscal retrenchment was achieved through a sharp curtailment of the social and education programs initiated by the Reconstructors. But the Conservatives also believed that railroad construction was essential to industrial growth, which they now accepted as a necessary balance to agriculture.

Even though their political oratory was shot through with references to the glories of the Old South and the Confederacy, the Redeemers had no difficulty in perfecting a working relationship with the Republican hierarchy in Washington. This was confirmed by the famous "Bargain of 1877," which resulted in the seating of the Republican presidential candidate, Rutherford B. Hayes, in return for the termination of Congressional Reconstruction in Louisiana and South Carolina. The bargain was struck when southern Democrats withdrew their support from their party's candidate, Samuel J. Tilden, who may have had the more legitimate claim to the contested election. "In effect," C. Vann Woodward wrote in *Reunion and Reaction,* "the Southerners were abandoning the cause of Tilden in exchange for control of two states, and the Republicans were abandoning the cause of the Negro in exchange for the peaceful possession of the Presidency." [5]

But Woodward contends that there was much more to the bargain than these surface political arrangements. The eastern financial community had able agents working behind the scenes whose longer-range interest was in restoring "safe" conservatives to power in the South to help head off the antibusiness sentiment beginning to surface all across the country in the wake of the scandals of the Grant administration. To this end there was an active canvass of the old Whig leaders who had reluctantly allied themselves with the secessionist Democrats. One of these was Gov. Augustus H. Garland of Arkansas, who in a private letter passed on to Hayes wrote off the struggle in Congress to resolve the presidential contest: "We all conclude we want no war, no trouble and deprecate every appearance of placing the South in any hostile attitude toward the federal government." [6]

5. C. Vann Woodward, *Reunion and Reaction* (Garden City, New York: Doubleday & Co., 1956), p. 6.

6. Woodward, *Reunion and Reaction,* p. 34.

Garland went on to the Senate after one term as governor and remained there until 1885, when he became attorney general in the cabinet of Grover Cleveland, a reward for faithful service in the coalition of southern Democrats and Republicans that contained the populist protest movement as it took shape in the industrial East and agrarian West.

In 1880 Arkansas had 822 miles of railroad; by 1890 the system had grown to 2,200 miles and constituted a transportation network that ran counter to the flow of the river systems. Steamboats would continue to transport passengers and freight into the twentieth century, but the competitive race had turned irrevocably against them. And much of the urban growth, minor though it still was, shifted from the river ports to new towns growing up along the railway lines.

The Reconstruction government had made a major effort to bring new settlers to Arkansas, creating the office of commissioner of state lands and immigration, which addressed invitations not only to fair-skinned foreigners but to black freedmen in the Deep South. A number of those who called themselves "exodusters" responded to literature that portrayed Arkansas as a new Africa, and carried the signature of the black political leader, William H. Grey, who became commissioner in 1871.

After Reconstruction the immigration drive was dominated by the railroads, whose proprietors were looking for settlers to buy and cultivate the land they had received by government grant. The first of a series of expenses-paid tours of the state for representatives of eastern and midwestern newspapers was organized in 1875, and there was an Arkansas display at the 1876 Philadelphia Centennial Exposition. At the height of this campaign the Saint Louis & Iron Mountain had three hundred full-time immigration agents in the field. The appeal was extended abroad through advertisements in European newspapers, and produced enough response to prompt the formation of an Immigration Aid Society at Little Rock, primarily supported by German settlers, some of whom were in the second and third generation and had become prominent in business affairs and municipal politics.

Towns with names like Stuttgart and Ulm now appeared on the map of Arkansas. A Polish settlement was established at

Marche near Little Rock, Bohemians came to Dardanelle, Sla-
vonian loggers worked in the forests, Italians abandoned their
first settlement in Chicot County to try grape culture at Tonti-
town in the northwest mountains. These, plus a sprinkling of
French, Swiss, Syrians, and Greeks, made up a foreign-born
population that grew from 5,126 in 1870 to 14,264 in 1890.
These immigrants, however, never accounted for as much as 2
percent of the total population, and except in a few isolated
colonies their language and old world customs rapidly disappeared.

There was some mining in the coalfields around Fort Smith
and some manufacturing in the larger towns, but the only major
new industry that could be attributed to the coming of the
railroads was attracted not by the promotion campaign but by
the enhanced availability of stands of virgin timber heretofore
cut only along streams large enough to accommodate logs
floated out in rafts. Northern lumber companies, having de-
pleted the forests from New England to Michigan, now turned
south to the Mississippi Valley. Armin T. Dressel, a forestry
expert, described what they found in Arkansas:

> The rolling hills were covered with huge loblolly and shortleaf pines
> that were four to five logs tall and averaged about 30 inches in
> diameter at breast height. . . . Associated with the stately pines
> were mature red oaks, white oaks, hickories, post oaks, sweet gums
> and various other hardwood species in lesser quantities. The
> hardwoods varied in size, but many were as large or larger in the
> diameter than the pine, but usually not as tall. . . . The virgin
> forest was open underneath and a man could ride horseback through
> the woods without having to duck brush. Deer could be sighted
> between the trees over one-quarter of a mile away.[7]

Arkansas's contribution to this development was cheap land
and cheap labor; by the 1880s the two largest landowners in
Grant County were the Saint Louis & Iron Mountain Railroad
and the Muskegon Lumber Company of Michigan. It was not
until well into this century that the cut-and-run practices of the
early loggers began to yield to recognition that even this bountiful timber supply was not limitless.

7. Armin T. Dressel, *Sheridan Headlight,* April 1, 1976.

A few local landowners managed to join forces with the out-of-state companies and gain a share of the profits. John F. Rutherford of Pine Bluff became one of Arkansas's first millionaires when he formed the Clio Lumber Company and sold it in 1909 for more than $1,500,000. And some of the out-of-state operators became permanent settlers: J. H. Hamlen & Sons, established in the cooperage trade at Portland, Maine, in the eighteenth century, began cutting white oak staves in Arkansas in the 1880s, and long since transferred its main office and principal operation to Little Rock under the direction of the current J. H. Hamlen. But these were the exceptions; most of the profits from the first clear-cutting were shipped out along with the lumber.

Supporting the effort to bring new settlers into the still underpopulated state, the *Gazette* proclaimed: "Arkansas is the home of the poor man, as well as of the capitalist. . . . No one need be without a home of his own in Arkansas. It can be had almost for the asking." [8] Most of those who responded to the opportunity for homesteading were in fact poor, and came from the older southern states which had supplied the basic stock. Although the state population passed a million in 1880 the great majority were still on the land. Little Rock, by far the largest city, grew from 13,000 in 1880 to 38,000 in 1900, when the state population stood at 1,311,000; but there were still only fifteen towns of more than 2,500 people, and only Little Rock, Pine Bluff, and Fort Smith counted more than 10,000.

The austere and gentlemanly Redeemers were no more successful in dealing with the state's fiscal problems than had been the Reconstructors. They could balance the budget by clamping down on public services to the point where there was growing political protest. But to maintain the drive for industrialization, they, no less than Powell Clayton, had to have access to the national money markets.

The Democrats inherited $10 million worth of railroad bonds, added to the $3.6 million financed by the Republicans to redeem

8. Jonathan James Wolfe, "Background of German Immigration," *Arkansas Historical Quarterly* 25 (Summer 1966): 155.

the defaulted bank securities. For the first few years of the new regime this bonded indebtedness was honored. The Democrats set up a State Board of Finance to deal with the problem, and added an item of their own—$280,000 to pay the expenses of their militia during the Brooks-Baxter War. But there was a growing popular movement for repudiation; the Holford issue was revived, and to this old grievance was added widespread resentment at being called upon to assume a debt incurred by carpetbaggers who had largely dissipated, and many believed stolen, the proceeds. By 1874 the inherited obligation was politically indefensible: "The credit had been lost through depreciation, the railroads had defaulted on the interest payment, and the state's debt had appeared as an annual curse." [9]

In 1877 the Arkansas Supreme Court ruled the Reconstruction railroad bonds unconstitutional, and in the course of that litigation two familiar figures were again center stage. Powell Clayton appeared as president of the defendant railroad, the Little Rock, Mississippi & Texas—which, as it turned out, intended to locate a station at "Linwood," the Clayton plantation below Pine Bluff. The adverse decision was written by the unreconstructed David Walker, who held that the election called to authorize the bonds did not meet the requirements of the state constitution.

The *New York Times* branded Justice Walker's grounds "technical and trumpery," and predicted that "having thus cast off its liabilities, of course Arkansas will by and by relieve itself still further." [10] But John D. Adams, a businessman who played a leading role in the effort to maintain the state's credit, wrote to Walker to assure him that inability to borrow money was not due to the court's decision, but to the legislature's penurious tax policies: "It could not be very encouraging to lenders to see a State reduce her taxes and borrow money to pay current expenses, then collect just enough taxes to pay that money back at the end of the year and leave the State in just the same financial condition as when she borrowed the year be-

9. Thompson, *Arkansas and Reconstruction*, p. 245.
10. Thompson, *Arkansas and Reconstruction*, p. 236.

fore." [11] The constitution was amended to certify the repudiation of several state issues, including the Holford bonds, and New York banks would not again accept Arkansas securities until 1917.

The Conservative leadership, with rare exceptions, was not equipped to deal with the likes of Jay Gould, who put together most of Arkansas's railway lines as he expanded his empire westward. They yielded their own and the state's long-range interests in return for immediate gain, and often didn't realize even that. The railroads set their own rates, paid few taxes, and where their interests were involved usually dominated state and local government. Arkansans belatedly came to recognize that their discriminatory freight rates actually nullified the vaunted drive for industrialization, confining Arkansas to the far less-rewarding role of producer of raw materials.

This condition continued for a hundred years after the Civil War. Arkansas has been described by the *Gazette's* economic analyst, Leland DuVall, as an economic colony bypassed by the industrial revolution. The system under which cotton dominated the state's economy was actually the antithesis of modern capitalism: "Sharecropping and renting were forms of voluntary serfdom in which the serfs were tied to the land by debt rather than decree." [12]

The planter, who occupied a place at the top of the social scale and received most of such benefits as the sharecrop system provided, nevertheless suffered a kind of bondage of his own, having to mortgage his crop each year to obtain operating funds at exorbitant interest rates justified by the high risk of the fluctuating cotton market—which saw prices fall from twenty-five cents a pound in 1868 to eleven cents in 1874 to five cents or less in 1894. C. Vann Woodward no doubt had his native state in mind when he concluded that over the years the crop lien system did more damage to the South than slavery.

Most Arkansans were caught in this debilitating trap. Cotton

11. Thompson, *Arkansas and Reconstruction,* p. 237.
12. Leland DuVall, *Arkansas: Colony and State* (Little Rock: Rose Publishing Co., 1973), p. 2.

cultivation spread beyond the lowland plantations to small farms ill-suited for it; to get credit a man had to pledge a cash crop, and cotton was the only recognized security. The sharecropper was irrevocably locked in; not having land, mules, or implements of his own he was dependent upon a plantation commissary or furnish merchant to advance him the means to feed his family while he made a crop, payment for these heavily marked-up goods having first call on his share of the proceeds when the cotton was sold.

Arkansas again had private banks, but their loans demanded not only high interest rates but backup security in the form of land that only the planters and the more substantial farmers could provide. Smallholders and renters, the one-horse or one-team farmers who were usually looking for something like two hundred dollars to get them from one harvest to the next, depended upon individual "hip-pocket" lenders who could usually be found whittling outside the general store in the crossroads towns. Leland DuVall has described these transactions:

> Interest rates were seldom a factor for the borrower. Percentage ranked along with trigonometry in the mysteries of higher mathematics and the farmer understood that he had to pay for the use of the money. The lenders, on the other hand . . . were particularly well versed in the science of discounting their loans. . . . All this meant that the cost of farm credit ranged "from 20 per cent to grand larceny." [13]

The debt-ridden, one-crop economy consigned the majority of Arkansans to subsistence on an annual income well below what would have been reckoned the poverty level in the growing American cities. Many were deprived of what those better situated came to regard as necessities—schooling, medical care, plumbing—and few of the so-called civilized amenities were available outside the larger towns. Yet these conditions were accepted as a valued way of life by those who settled in the mountains, where, by circumstance or choice, or a combination of both, there flourished an early counterculture. They raised or

13. DuVall, *Arkansas: Colony and State,* p. 27.

hunted their own food, grew tobacco and made whiskey to sustain their bad habits, entertained each other with homemade music and oft-told tales, drew solace from the old-time religion, and generally looked upon change as a threat to their ordained way of life. Their situation, sustained by their own stubborn pride, was significantly different from that of equally impoverished lowlanders, the black and white sharecroppers who accepted economic bondage as the only means they knew that would permit them to cling to the edge of subsistence.

There can be no doubt that the severely constricted agricultural economy took a heavy human toll, visiting physical disability and an equally crippling lack of will upon succeeding generations of blacks and poor whites. But there were others of both races, not much better off in a material way, for whom the land provided a benison, sustaining an optimism and vitality transmitted from parents to their progeny during all the long years of stagnation that followed the lost war.

If one can rely on the literature of the period it must be concluded that the bluebird of happiness nested in the backwoods of Arkansas at least as frequently as in the crowded neighborhoods of the growing industrial cities. There, too, determined parents managed to send bright children to school, and on to the towns where opportunities were deemed greater. A remarkable number of these, attaining affluence and status in urban society, looked back upon their growing up, with all its hazards and privations, as a genuine idyll.

One of these, John Quincy Wolf, was born in 1864 in a one-room log cabin on the White River opposite Calico Rock. Orphaned at ten, he was raised by an uncle and aunt in a nearby hill section called the Leatherwoods. Over the years Wolf's childless foster parents took in thirteen other orphans, mostly of their own blood. These youngsters constituted the only work force regularly employed on Uncle William Swan's two-horse farm. His crops were oats, millet, corn, clover, cowpeas, wheat, tobacco, and a few acres of cotton; there was also a hundred-tree fruit orchard, strawberries, raspberries, vegetables, beehives, and six to ten milk cows. A small herd of beef cattle and a drove of razorback hogs foraged in the forested range behind his own cleared acres. "In the spring," Wolf wrote,

"Uncle sold from ten to twenty-five head of cattle to Missouri buyers, and in the fall two or three bales of cotton, which brought in more than enough money for the family needs." [14]

The rest of that bountiful harvest went to supply the foodstuff that sustained the family, a constant stream of visitors, and the indigent who made claim on the Swans' charity. Wolf's memory overflows with rapt descriptions of tidal waves of pure cream, huge country biscuits made of flour from waterground wheat soaked in black gravy from home-cured ham, vegetables emerging fresh and flavorful from underground storage in dead of winter, an endless array of jams, jellies, and preserves, the tantalizing sights and smells when hog-killing time came with first frost, the mystique of game skinned and cooked by the hunter who bagged it, fish popped in the skillet minutes away from clear, cold streams rushing down from the Ozarks.

Life in the Leatherwoods is an account of the maturation of a boy growing up in a literal land of milk and honey. And, on the gastronomic front at least, it contrasts sharply with the memories of Jessie Rose, daughter of one of Arkansas's most eminent citizens, Judge U. M. Rose. She recalled the limitations of the Little Rock cuisine in the 1890s: "Bear meat was not really good—it had a sweetish and very greasy taste, but there was so little variety in the long winter months, with shipped vegetables undreamed of and endless turnips and onions palling, that we ate bear meat whenever it was in the market just because it was a change." [15]

Wolf's aunt and uncle saw that he got to the local subscription schools, such as they were, and sent him finally to the academy at Mountain Home. And they did not stand in his way when he came to manhood and in 1886 signed on the steamboat *Josie Harry,* still defying the encroaching railroads with a regular run up the White River. He settled, finally, down the valley at Batesville, where he earned his living as a banker and pursued his avocations as author and naturalist until his death in

14. John Quincy Wolf, *Life in the Leatherwoods* (Memphis: Memphis State University Press, 1974), p. 27.

15. *Arkansas Gazette,* Oct. 25, 1964.

1949, drawing praise from such a literary titan as H. L. Mencken, the scourge of the Bible Belt.

Wolf could hardly be called typical of his generation, but neither was he unique; many less-articulate Arkansans would concur in his summing up:

> I know too well how abbreviated was my schooling and how limited
> were my early opportunities for broadening myself. . . . I believe
> that the narrow life I led during my childhood and youth has
> increased many times my appreciation of the world that has
> unfolded for me during the ensuing years. In the quiet of the hills,
> far from the noise and the rush of cities, I learned to look at
> commonplace things large and small and see whatever was special
> about them.[16]

16. Wolfe, *Life in the Leatherwoods*, p. 147.

12

The Thrust from Below

*C*RAVELING through the South and West in the 1880s on assignment for *Harper's Monthly Magazine,* Charles Dudley Warner found Arkansas's capital city free of any residual trace of the brawling frontier. "It has the settled, temperate, orderly society of an Eastern town, but democratic in its habits, and with a cordial hospitality which is more provincial than fashionable," he wrote. He was pleased to hear a good chamber music concert of stringed instruments, and he concluded that when adequate street improvements were made Little Rock would be a beautiful city. Warner was struck by the absence of visible scars from the recent unpleasantness: "The street cars and railways make no discrimination as to color of passenger. Everywhere I went I noticed that the intercourse between the two races was friendly." [1]

This surface tranquility was the handiwork of the Redeemers, who employed the popularity earned in their rout of the Reconstructors to mortar into place a one-party political system that would endure for nearly a century. Their leaders were of the broadcloth gentry, and their hallmark was civility. As the old Whig label disappeared, and the generic term Conservative which had served during Reconstruction lost currency, capital-D Democrat became the mark of status and respectability. The Republicans, with black support, could still muster a third of the

1. Margaret Ross, "Chronicles of Arkansas," *Arkansas Gazette,* Nov. 2, 1958.

state's vote, but socially they were beyond the pale. When Sam Collyer met Patsy McGraw in Arkansas's first prize fight of record, the *Gazette* scorned the match as "the first time two men ever deliberately concluded to maul each other for money," and took due note of the fact that the one hundred spectators were Republicans: "No Democrats present except your correspondent, who is sorry." [2]

Racism was not a primary factor in this political dispensation. The Democrats accepted as their end of the bargain of 1877 an obligation to protect the newly won civil rights of the former slaves. They made no move to limit the vote, but sought, with some success, to create a black constituency of their own. Under what was called the "fusion principle," white Democratic leaders in the plantation belt commonly got together with black Republicans to trade out places on the ballot so that candidates on each side would be unopposed. Under this arrangement there were blacks in the Arkansas legislature, many county courthouses, and the Little Rock City Council until late in the century.

The tradition of the conservative leadership called for benign tolerance of all the lesser orders, not only the freedmen but the poor whites who had marched into battle under the Confederate officers who now took command of the Democratic party. So long as the old soldiers reciprocated they could dominate local and district party conventions, and finally the state convention, so that hand-picked Democratic nominees for key offices would be virtually certain to prevail against Republican opponents in the general election.

Caught up, as they were, in the drive for industrialization, the Democratic leaders supported the railroad and banking interests at the expense of their natural constituency, taking a niggardly approach to public services while they extended privilege to the financiers and promoters they believed would transform the state for the benefit of all its citizens. The theology of the Gilded Age, which now prevailed in Washington and in every state capital across the land, proclaimed a coincidence between altruism and self-interest. If this was accepted as a proper standard

2. Ross, "Chronicles of Arkansas," *Arkansas Gazette,* Aug. 14, 1966.

of conduct it followed that many political leaders found a considerable overlap between their public and private obligations.

In Arkansas, a significant number of the Redeemers, having come to power as symbols of rectitude, succumbed to temptation. Three Confederate heroes left the state treasurer's office under a cloud. Col. Robert C. Newton, commander of the Redemptionist army in the Brooks-Baxter War, was involved in a bank failure that cost the state $22,000. Gen. Thomas J. Churchill, who became governor in 1880, was accused by a legislative committee of having incurred a shortage of $300,000 during his tenure as treasurer, and was ordered by the supreme court to repay $80,522 to the state. And Maj. William E. Woodruff, Jr., who made the *Gazette* the voice of the political establishment, was charged with a shortage of almost $150,000 and, although acquitted on criminal charges, had to refund more than $90,000.

Such lapses were not confined to the upper reaches of the Democratic hierarchy, but were widespread among the county courthouses. Newspapers in the early 1880s were studded with items involving forgery, perjury, defalcations, and embezzlements; and grand juries regularly complained of inefficiency and waste. A representative sampling included findings of mis- and malfeasance against the county judge, sheriff, and treasurer in Franklin County; court action against the sheriff and tax collector in Washington County; election of an assessor in Desha County who was wanted by the sheriff for grand larceny; and the loss to Ouachita County of $8,000 when it was discovered that the late treasurer had defaulted and his bondsman was "both dead and insolvent." [3]

Thus disillusionment was added to the economic dislocations besetting back-country Arkansans who cast their lot with the Democrats. If evidence that affairs were going from bad to worse was not readily visible in Little Rock, it was inescapable in the county seats. The only thriving "business" the *Waldron Reporter* could locate in Scott County in 1882 was that carried

3. Francis Clark Elkins, "Arkansas Farmers Organize for Action: 1882–1884," *Arkansas in the Gilded Age* (Little Rock: Rose Publishing Co. 1976), p. 22. This is an anthology edited by Waddy William Moore and made up principally of articles reprinted from the *Arkansas Historical Quarterly.*

on by justices of the peace: "From all directions we hear of at-
tachments for debt, many for rent, closing out under mortgages
for supplies, suits on notes, filing schedules for exempt property, etc. All the direct result of the ruinous credit system, and
raising cotton to sell below the cost of production." [4] A letter to
the editor of the *Fort Smith Elevator* made the connection between distress in the countryside and Democratic political rhetoric, calling upon voters to elect competent, honest men and ignore the "bloody shirt, secession, war and reconstruction
nonsense some are still preaching." [5]

Grass-roots political reaction was inevitable in a constituency
that at least enjoyed the forms of representative government.
"With blacks at the bottom and most whites little if any above
them, they lived year in and year out in debtor's peonage at a
level of privation and humiliation that was 'un-American' by
any reckoning," C. Vann Woodward has written. "Classes nor-
mally and natively conservative were ripe for radicalization." [6]

The first farmers' protest movement in Arkansas was organized by a patrician planter, John T. Jones, who was graduated
from the University of Virginia in 1833 and three years later set
himself up on a plantation near Helena. In 1872 he applied to
the recently organized National Grange for an Arkansas charter.
The *Helena World* applauded the new organization: "The merchant, the politician, the speculator, . . . have not been slow to
avail themselves of a power which, collected even from feeble
sources, is, when agitated, well nigh irresistible. . . . The hus-
bandmen alone have not manifested the disposition, if they have
possessed the power, to organize. They have been beggars who
have received the crumbs that have fallen from the tables of
others." [7]

The Grange had the trappings of a fraternal order. Its program
called for self-education and mutual assistance, which seemed

4. Elkins, "Arkansas Farmers," p. 21.

5. Elkins, "Arkansas Farmers," p. 23.

6. C. Vann Woodward, "The Promise of Populism," *New York Review of Books*
23 (Oct. 28, 1976): 29.

7. Granville Daniel Davis, "The Granger Movement in Arkansas," *Arkansas in the
Gilded Age*, pp. 5, 6.

to point vaguely toward the formation of co-operatives to buy farm supplies and market crops. But since it stressed co-operation with existing commercial interests, the political leadership saw nothing inherently alarming in the Granger movement. In 1873 the *Gazette* offered an admonitory blessing: "Throughout the state we note that this organization is rapidly taking root, and we watch its progress with deepest interest. We trust that politics will find no footing in its counsels, and that being the case, the organization may become one from which our whole state may reap the largest benefits." [8]

At its high point in 1875 the Arkansas Grange had 20,471 members in 631 chapters located in more than half the state's seventy-five counties, and John T. Jones had been elevated to the post of master of the National Grange. Within four years most of these chapters disappeared as the leadership provided no effective program of action to sustain the hope it had kindled. In 1882 a tougher-fibered agricultural movement came into being. William Walker Tedford, a self-educated rural schoolteacher and Cumberland Presbyterian minister, led seven Prairie County farmers in the formation of the Wattensas Farmers Club, proclaiming the need for grass-roots organization to fight the monopolies he charged with oppressing the farmers. Within a year Arkansans were flocking to join the organization, rechristened the Agricultural Wheel. This time the enemy was clearly identified: the railroads, the financial interests, the furnish merchants, and the Democratic political organizations they dominated.

The Wheel, too, had lodge-style overtones. The organization's name was borrowed from the prophet Ezekiel, and its hymn had the ring of the church militant:

> *Come all ye sunburnt sons of toil,*
> *Arise from thine oppression;*
> *'Tis true we till the stubborn soil,*
> *But a highway to progression,*
> *Which enemies cannot conceal*
> *Is opened by this mighty Wheel.* [9]

8. Davis, "Granger Movement," p. 7.
9. Elkins, "Arkansas Farmers," pp. 27, 28.

By 1884 there was a Grand State Wheel, led by E. R. Mc-Pherson, with nearly 5,000 members in 114 subordinate Wheels. As the spokes spread out from the hub the Wheel absorbed other farm organizations that had sprung up across Arkansas, including the numerically larger Brothers of Freedom, which had rallied the farmers in the northwest section. The Brothers movement was the product of mixed reaction to the Greenback party, which had a brief flurry in Arkansas, combining with the Republicans in 1880 to run a candidate for governor who received 31,284 votes, 27 percent of the total. The idea that monetary reform might provide a means of breaking through the grinding credit system made the demand for something less than hard money a dominant issue in all the agrarian movements. But the upland farmers were put off by the Greenbackers' courting of the freedmen's vote, which was considered an unacceptable brand of radical politics in the hills; the Brothers' creed was described as a blend of Scripture, the Declaration of Independence, and Greenback economic theory. The organization proscribed direct political action, preaching a self-help gospel that called for breaking through the one-crop economy by means of a diversified "hog and hominy" farm operation that would supply the family's needs and free the farmer of dependence upon cotton-based credit.

The Brothers of Freedom claimed 40,000 members when it merged with the Wheel in 1885, and its leader, Isaac Mc-Cracken of Johnson County, became grand president. The merger pushed the organization toward direct political action, and the *Arkansas Daily Democrat* warned: "All the old enemies of the Democratic Party—the men who have helped issue bonds and impose burdensome taxes in the past, and who know that under their true name, Republicans, they could never come to the front, are now zealous and loud mouthed 'Brothers' and 'Wheelers.' " [10]

In 1886 the Wheelers, still divided internally on the issue of direct political action, half-heartedly entered a candidate for governor under a Labor-Wheel banner, and ran a poor third. The percentage breakdown of that vote pointed clearly in the di-

10. Elkins, "Arkansas Farmers," p. 49.

rection of the kind of coalition politics the Redeemers had used to unseat the Reconstructors. In the election of 1888 the Wheeler leadership made a deal with Powell Clayton. In the last week of April 1888, the Arkansas Union Labor party was organized at Little Rock, under the chairmanship of Isaac Mc-Cracken, now president of the National Wheel with a membership of 500,000 across the South. The Republican state convention, for the first time since the party's founding, decided not to enter a slate of candidates for state office.

The platform of the Union Labor party was a set of "demands" adopted by the Wheel in 1887, calling for regulation of railroads and utilities, with forfeiture of all earnings of more than 6 percent; state taxation to maintain rural roads; laws to provide for the sanctity of the ballot box; levy of county-wide rather than district school taxes; and prohibition against hiring armed men by corporations. These demands also were presented to the Democrats when they convened in May to nominate a Lonoke planter, Col. James P. Eagle. The Wheelers were ignored, and the *Gazette* sought to soften the blow by pointing out that the Democrats' nomination of a farmer in itself was "recognition of that great body of our people, the tillers of the soil." [11] The Wheelers replied that on Colonel Eagle's place the tilling was done by tenants who had to trade at the plantation store, a reaction that prompted the colonel to point out that at least he had never taken a crop lien.

The Union Labor party nominated for governor an obscure one-legged Confederate private, C. M. Norwood, and by June there was no doubt that he would have the support of the Wheelers, the incipient trade union movement represented by the Knights of Labor, and all the Republicans Powell Clayton could muster. The *Gazette* reprinted from the *Chicago Tribune* an interview with Judge John A. Williams of Jefferson County who, attending the Republican national convention, "talked interestingly about the possibility of a combination that would end the Democratic dynasty in rock-ribbed Arkansas. They expect to

11. Clifton Paisley, "The Political Wheelers and Arkansas' Election of 1888," *Arkansas in the Gilded Age*, p. 61.

do so through that queerly-named organization known as the 'Wheel'.'' The *Gazette* thundered: ''The mask has been torn off, and the authors of the crimes of the Reconstruction era stand forth in bold relief.'' [12]

The National Union Labor party sent in its presidential candidate, A. J. Streeter, to stump the state on behalf of the colorless Norwood. Colonel Eagle and his backers concentrated on splitting the unnatural alliance between the traditionally Democratic farmers and the Republicans. The Democratic strategy succeeded, but only barely; Eagle won by 99,214 to 84,213, and there was ample reason to believe that the fifteen-thousand vote majority was accounted for in substantial part by widespread fraud. There was at least one physical casualty of the 1888 campaign, John M. Clayton, younger brother of the Republican leader, who was assassinated while investigating irregularities in his race for Congress in the Second District; his contest was upheld posthumously by the Republican Congress, as was the challenge of the Wheeler candidate in the First District.

Two years later the Wheel had been merged into the National Farmers Alliance, which was taking on the Democratic leadership all across the South, and the coalition again tried for the governorship but lost by a bigger margin, 106,267 to 85,181. The election of 1888 marked the high-water mark of the agrarian challenge, and in its wake the alarmed Democratic leadership perfected the one-party system by eliminating the factor that gave coalitionists the prospect of achieving a statewide majority—the black vote.

Negro-baiting, as a means of activating rural voters in the name of white supremacy, made its first appearance in Arkansas nearly a quarter of a century after the end of the Civil War. The old Redeemers were clearly uncomfortable with it, and in the Eagle-Norwood campaign the *Gazette* raised the issue by indirection, quoting a Republican candidate in Jackson County who was alleged to have said that ''the time is not far distant

12. Paisley, ''Political Wheelers,'' p. 62.

when the nigger and the white man would eat side by side at the same table and sleep side by side in the same bed." [13]

In 1890 the Democratic leadership took its first overt anti-Negro position, calling for Jim Crow segregation of the races on the railroads. Prior to that time the civil rights act passed in 1873 by the last Reconstruction legislature had been allowed to stand; it barred racial segregation in common carriers, hotels, saloons, restaurants, and "places of public amusement." How far this policy actually applied in practice may be open to some doubt, but it is clear that blacks moved freely in many areas subsequently barred to them. The black carpetbag leader, Mifflin Gibbs, testified in his autobiography, *Shadow and Light,* that Little Rock was more liberal in its treatment of freedmen than any other southern city, and cited the admission of blacks to the board of trade, real estate exchange, bar, lyceum, and professional and literary societies. As late as 1897 the Ex-Slaves Association staged its annual jamboree at Little Rock's West End Park, which also was the site of the Confederate reunion.

The Separate Coach Act of 1891 required "equal but separate and sufficient" railroad passenger coaches and waiting rooms. The test for determining who was to be segregated was "a visible and distinct admixture of African blood." There was some talk of the need for protecting respectable whites against noisy, drunken, insolent, and smelly blacks, but for the most part the gentlemanly Redeemers seemed almost apologetic in arguing for the measure. Its Senate sponsor said he had drafted his bill in conformity to the Mississippi coach law, and the *Gazette* emphasized that the United States Supreme Court's 1891 "separate but equal" ruling upholding the statute confirmed that "such separation of the races as is contemplated by the bill is not 'caste or class legislation.' " [14]

The blacks saw it differently. A protest meeting that drew more than 600 persons to the Negro First Baptist Church in Little Rock adopted a resolution branding the proposed law as "the special insult, contumely and imposition of a certain well

---

13. Paisley, "Political Wheelers," p. 70.

14. John William Graves, "The Arkansas Separate Coach Law of 1891," *Arkansas in the Gilded Age,* p. 83.

known class of white persons." Prof. J. A. Booker of the black Arkansas Baptist College proposed as an alternative the provision of first- and second-class service without regard to race as a means of protecting all respectable citizens against uncouth travelers. Dr. J. H. Smith, a dentist, warned: "Ignorance is contagious. To force the better negroes into contact with the more degraded would be to force the race backward." The *Gazette* reported the meeting fully, finding it "characterized throughout by conservatism and eloquence." [15]

The sole black member of the senate, George W. Bell of Desha County, also took a constructive line when he spoke against the measure, telling his colleagues how he boasted of Arkansas's good record in race relations when traveling in the North, pleading with them not to destroy the state's reputation for just and equitable treatment of the black minority. On the house side, John G. Lucas of Jefferson County, one of ten blacks still serving there, warned that if Arkansas were "yoked to the crimson soil of Mississippi, she shall be as incapable of advancement as is a fixed star to alter its course." He took note of the openness of existing residential patterns, arguing that it would be as absurd to separate the races on the railroads as it would be "to require all white people to live in one particular portion of our cities and the colored people in the other portion." And he attacked head-on the essential hypocrisy of the proposed statute:

> Is it true, as charged, that we use less of soap and God's pure water than other people, that it is sought to isolate us from other fellow citizens? . . . Why, some of our Democratic papers have said that the more money, intelligence and gentility, the more objectionable the negro. Which is the truth? Do our white friends demand this law that they may not be compelled to travel in the same car with the former class? Or is it the constant growth of a more refined, intelligent, and I might say more perfumed class, that grow more and more obnoxious as they more nearly approximate to our white friends' habits and plane of life?

As the bill moved inexorably to passage an amendment was offered to include street cars, and the *Gazette* recorded Lucas's

15. Graves, "Arkansas Separate Coach Law," p. 85.

ironic response, in which he asserted that he had no desire to commingle with whites, and would even favor a line dividing the sidewalk between the two races. In fact, he said, he would "like to see an end put to all intercourse between white and colored people by day, and especially by night." [16] Only one white senator and two white representatives, all Republicans, joined the black legislators in voting against the measure.

The arrival of Jim Crow in Arkansas presaged the end of active black participation in the political process. In the election of 1892 the coalition between the Republicans and the agrarian reformers broke down; the Republicans entered their own slate, and the rural dissidents gathered under the new Populist banner on the march in the South and West. The Arkansas People's party tried to keep the door open; at the initial convention the 170 delegates from fifty-two counties included eighty-two Confederate veterans, thirty-two ex-Union soldiers, and eleven blacks. But that grouping could not hold in the face of the rising tide of white xenophobia. The *Arkadelphia Siftings* correctly prophesied: "This is a white man's country, and white men are going to rule it, and when the third party opened its arms to the Negro at its State convention, it invited its certain death at the polls next fall." [17] The Populist candidate got slightly less than 20 percent of the vote; that total held in 1894 when the candidate identified himself as "Moderate Populist"; in 1896 the percentage was down to 9.87, and the decline continued until in 1900 the percentage was only 2.74. Through these years the Republican percentage ranged from 25 to 30 percent and included what remained of the black vote.

In 1891 the entrenched Democrats put through an election reform measure which required the secret "Australian" ballot and provided that illiterates, who previously could have friends or party workers prepare a ballot for them, must have their tickets marked by precinct judges—who, to preserve secrecy, were required to clear all other electors from the polling place. How this worked in practice was celebrated in an 1892 Demo-

16. Graves, "Arkansas Separate Coach Law," pp. 89, 90, 91.
17. Graves, "Arkansas Separate Coach Law," p. 97.

cratic campaign ballad sung to the tune of the Confederate marching song, "The Bonnie Blue Flag":

> The Australian ballot works like a charm,
> It makes them think and scratch,
> And when a negro gets a ballot
> He has certainly got his match.
>
> *Chorus*
> *Hurrah! Hurrah! for Arkansas Hurrah!*
> *And when we elect Old Grover*
> *We will make them kick and paw.*
>
> They go into the booth alone
> Their ticket to prepare.
> And as soon as five minutes are out
> They have got to git from there.—*Chorus*
>
> They then next to the Judge applies
> With a little tale of woe,
> And of course his ticket is well prepared,
> Which someone is bound to know.—*Chorus* [18]

There also were white illiterates and many of these simply stopped voting because of embarrassment at having to declare their deficiency publicly. This was a matter of little concern to Democrats of the Bourbon persuasion. The *Pine Bluff Commercial* forthrightly declared: "The ignorant and uneducated whites and blacks cannot vote the ticket, which ought to be, and is a blessing to the state, for ignorance should never rule a great commonwealth like Arkansas." [19] In the 1892 election a constitutional amendment was passed adopting a poll tax and requiring a receipt, which identified the holder by race, in order to obtain a ballot. Between 1890 and 1894 these measures combined to reduce the total vote by some 65,000, one-third of the total.

In 1898 the Arkansas Democratic Central Committee added to these formidable barriers the ultimate means of disfranchisement—ordering the system of nominating candidates by convention replaced by a "popular" party primary election limited to

18. Graves, "Arkansas Separate Coach Law," p. 103.
19. Graves, "Arkansas Separate Coach Law," p. 104.

whites. Thus the only effective means of political participation open to blacks was membership in the Republican party, and while they could still vote under federal protection in general elections, tight Democratic control of the election machinery rendered this meaningless. Powell Clayton, who certainly qualified as an expert in such matters, characterized the process: "Here the Democrats shuffle, cut and deal the cards, then look in both hands and say, 'Walk up, Mr. Republican, and vote,' and the Republican has mighty little chance for the jack pot." [20]

In following this course Arkansas adapted to the pattern spreading across the whole of the South. Disfranchisement of the blacks had its inception in the real threat to the conservative establishment posed by the coalition of Republicans and agrarian reformers, and it appears that this was less a result than a cause of the obsession with white supremacy that was to become a determinant in elections to follow. A student of the Arkansas experience, John William Graves, observed that there were some who hoped that elimination of Negro participation in the political process would have the constructive result of enabling white men to divide on fundamental economic issues. The result, however, was the reverse: "Embittered by the way the race issue had been used to shipwreck their movement, many Populists irrationally turned against the Negro and used him as a scapegoat for their disappointments and frustrations. Democrats skillfully exploited these feelings by simultaneously welcoming ex-Populists back into the ranks and excluding Negroes from voting in the primaries." [21]

Thus the mold was set for the spectacular but essentially sterile one-party politics that prevailed in Arkansas until well past World War II.

20. Graves, "Arkansas Separate Coach Law," p. 106.
21. Graves, "Arkansas Separate Coach Law," p. 111.

13

Red Necks and Silver Tongues

 have never been called by anybody a violent partisan,"
Arkansas's first elected governor proclaimed in an 1836
campaign circular. Denying charges that his kinfolk had
benefitted unduly from his activities as surveyor general of the
territory, James Sevier Conway went on to say that he had
formed a political alliance with other members of the Dynasty
only because he knew them to be honest and honorable men.
"On the subject of national politics," the staunch Jacksonian
continued, "if I have ever been suspected of being anything but
a true Democratic Republican, I have not been apprised of such
suspicion. I have been taught it from my infancy, and am now
teaching it to my children." [1]

For the next century and a quarter, except for the decade of
Reconstruction, the Democratic banner flew over the statehouse.
Political organization was more a rallying of the clan than a sys-
tematic effort to sort out men of like mind on the issues of the
day. And the election campaign became a public entertainment
which usually yielded its highest rewards to members of the
broadcloth gentry who sounded like common men—or at least
said better than they could the things common men wanted to
hear.

It was not a milieu in which a sober man of rigid principle
had much chance of success. David Walker, the straitlaced

1. Margaret Ross, "Chronicles of Arkansas," *Arkansas Gazette,* Jan. 10, 1960.

Whig who served with distinction on the state's highest court, was repeatedly frustrated when he entered elective politics. Campaigning for Congress, Judge Walker could not bring himself to indulge in the activities that ordinarily accompanied a backwoods political rally—dram-drinking and a shooting match with a beef carcass as the prize. His opponent, Archibald Yell, was eternally ready to get his bets down and enter the match; when he won he sent the beef to the neediest widow in the neighborhood, bought a jug of whiskey, and invited all hands to celebrate his victory; when he lost he bought a jug to solace his backers. "Those attainments and achievements fulfilled the estimate of congressional qualifications in the opinion of the sovereign electors," a contemporary observer wrote, noting that Yell did just as well in the role of Scripture-quoter and hymn-singer when the campaign trail coincided with a brush arbor revival meeting.[2]

Political oratory is a forensic art, and the successful practitioner requires an enemy against whom he can unite his followers. For Arkansas's silver-tongued champions there were first the abolitionists, then the invading United States Army and the alien Reconstructors; in the postwar years all these were conveniently wrapped up in a partisan package labeled Republican. Since the Democratic leaders honestly believed that an elitist effort to develop the state's industrial potential was in the best interest of all its citizens, they had no problems of conscience in waving their own version of the bloody shirt while embracing the conservative, free-enterprise philosophy that prevailed everywhere in the United States in the decades after the Civil War. They were not blind to the Darwinian effect of unbridled capitalism in a poor, defeated agrarian province; they could sympathize with the plight of small farmers and tenants caught in the squeeze of exorbitant credit costs and declining commodity prices; but they could not yield to the angry thrust of populist demands without abandoning their faith that governance could only be entrusted to prudent men—that is, to men like themselves.

2. Ross, "Chronicles of Arkansas," *Arkansas Gazette*, Oct. 17, 1960.

In the years of agrarian revolt the gap between political rhetoric and the realities of public policy steadily widened. When the Democrats reinforced the fading memories of Reconstruction with the racist appeal of white supremacy they were arousing the farmers against an enemy that did not exist—for there was never any real competitive threat to the poor whites from the blacks who shared their misery. In the hands of unprincipled politicians, however, the race issue could be used to help denature the wrath the white masses continued to direct against the conservative establishment; when a candidate turned up who could solidify a personal following it was usually possible, with his tacit consent, to render him effectively impotent in critical areas of economic policy.

Most of those who rode the agrarian protest to office caricatured the movement's principles and came to be treated in contemporary national context as picturesque clowns. The man who played this role in Arkansas was a well-born lawyer endowed with a hallowed name that served him well, although this Jefferson Davis claimed no kin to the original. In 1888, not long out of the University of Arkansas and Vanderbilt University Law School, Davis entered politics on the Bourbon side, standing as the youngest Democratic presidential elector in the election that narrowly turned back the Wheelers. In his law practice at Russellville, his first name shortened to Jeff, he acquired an intimate knowledge of the grievances of the upland farmers, and perfected a unique ability to define them in terms that identified him as their champion. "The agrarians never won in Arkansas," Clifton Paisley wrote, "but Democrats learned to speak their language. None spoke it better than Jeff Davis." [3]

In his first elective office, attorney general, Davis apparently made an effort to fulfill his pledge to lead a crusade against the "high-collared roosters" who controlled the business affairs of the state. When the general assembly in 1899 passed an antitrust act he initiated prosecutions he promised would run all foreign corporations out of Arkansas. The state supreme court nullified

3. Clifton Paisley, "The Political Wheelers and Arkansas' Election of 1888," *Arkansas in the Gilded Age* (Little Rock: Rose Publishing Co., 1976), p. 74.

the effort, but this rhetorical trust-busting provided the impetus that took Jeff Davis to the governorship in 1900, kept him there for an unprecedented three terms, and allowed him to finish out his life as United States senator.

It can't be said that the poor farmers of Arkansas were any better off as a result of Jeff Davis's spectacular career, but he surely offered balm for their psychic wounds. "This is a true contest between the silk stocking crowd and the one-gallus brigade," he would proclaim as he mounted the stump, shedding his lawyer's jim-swinger coat to display a single strap holding up his trousers. His invective against city folk in general, and the leading newspapers in particular, left an oratorical heritage his successors on the hustings employed to good effect for more than fifty years after his death. Margaret Ross culled these nuggets from published and typescript versions of typical Jeff Davis campaign speeches:

To sustain his theme of citified prodigality, he cited the purchase of the site of a new penitentiary at Little Rock:

> Five thousand dollars! Fifteen acres of land! That land is so poor that two drunken men couldn't raise a difficulty upon it. It is so poor that you could not raise an umbrella on it. It is so poor that you have to manure it to make brick out of it.

The newspapers, most notably the *Gazette*, were favorite targets, and he frequently used them interchangeably to suit the locale:

> The *Helena World* says that I am a carrot-haired, red-faced, loud-mouthed, strong-limbed, ox-driving mountaineer lawyer . . . that I am a friend to the fellow that brews forty-rod bug juice back in the mountains. . . . I have a little boy, God bless him. If I find out that boy is a smart boy I will go and make a preacher out of him; if I find he is not so smart a boy I am going to make a lawyer out of him; if I find he has not a bit of sense upon earth, I am going to make an editor out of him and send him to Little Rock to edit the *Arkansas Democrat*. . . .

> I see the *Gazette* agent out there in the audience giving out that old red harlot, the *Arkansas Gazette*. I had rather be caught with a dead buzzard under my arm, or a dead polecat.

His speciality was reversing the epithets scornfully applied to country people so as to make them virtually terms of endearment, as in this blanket invitation extended after he was in the governor's office:

> If you red-necks or hill-billies ever come to Little Rock be sure and come to see me—come to my house. Don't go to the hotels or wagon-yards, but come to my house and make it your home. If I am not there tell my wife who you are, that you are my friend and belong to the sunburned sons of toil. Tell her to give you some hog jowl and turnip-greens. She may be busy making soap, but that will be all right; you will be properly cared for and it will save you a hotel bill.

Although his salary as governor was not exactly a starvation wage, he pictured himself as just another impoverished victim of the trusts:

> Old Armour and Cudahy never raised a sow and pigs in their lives. Yet the prices of meat are so high that I can hardly buy breakfast bacon in Little Rock enough to support my family. I just buy one slice, hang it up by a long string, and let each one of my kids jump up and grease their mouths and go to bed.

And when he was himself accused of playing fast and loose with the public trust he usually managed to turn the tables, as in this response when a patrician opponent made an issue of his granting pardons wholesale:

> Judge Wood said the other day . . . that any old woman could get a pardon at my office who came there crying. . . . God bless you, old mothers in Israel; God bless their prayers and their tears; and mothers, when you offer up your devotion tonight if you can spare one moment, list a prayer for this pardoning governor of Arkansas. If you don't want your boys pardoned, don't come crying around my office.[4]

The most innocent countryman made some discount for Jeff Davis's broadaxe irony; no one really believed that Mrs. Davis made soap in the backyard down at Little Rock while her chil-

---

4. Ross, "Chronicles of Arkansas," *Arkansas Gazette,* July 3, 1960.

dren snapped at worn-out bacon rinds in the kitchen, and the governor's residence was never overwhelmed by sunburned sons of toil accepting his offer of free room and board. But his devoted followers made an even heavier discount for anything said against him, no matter how well documented, and so he became impervious to counterattack, having discredited the press in advance. In a rudimentary sense he built what could be called a political machine, dispensing patronage to legislators and courthouse politicians who could deliver votes. But his principal reliance was on his personal appeal; his influence never effectively extended beyond the office he held, and it dissipated with his death.

The heritage from the agrarian revolt was a loose factionalism held together by nothing more tangible than mutual prejudice between poor farmers and townsfolk, which may have been rooted in a genuine conflict of interest but rarely produced programmatic issues that survived from one election to the next. The fortunes of political combat shifted back and forth between these vague groupings; when Jeff Davis died in office in 1912 the lame-duck governor, George W. Donaghey, dispensed poetic justice by appointing as his short-term successor one of the most conspicuous symbols of his opposition, the genteel editor of the *Arkansas Gazette,* J. N. Heiskell.

Charles Hillman Brough, who served as governor from 1917 to 1921, represented a peculiarly contrasting strain in Arkansas politics, coming directly to the office from the faculty of the University of Arkansas, where he had served as professor of economics since 1903. Jeff Davis had casually plunged the university into partisan politics when, in 1905, he let it be known that he wanted Pres. Henry S. Hartzog fired. The board of trustees, on which the governor then sat as chairman, promptly obliged. Robert A. Leflar, who wrote the university's centennial history, found that the action was taken in preparation for Davis's impending race for the United States Senate, in which he planned to unseat an incumbent presumed to be popular in the Fayetteville area: "He had nothing against President Hartzog, but Hartzog would not help him against Senator Berry, and someone else could.'' [5] That someone was John N. Tillman, circuit judge for the northwest district, who retained the university presidency until 1917 when he resumed his active political career and served five terms in Congress, blazing a trail that would be followed a generation later by J. William Fulbright.

Brough, who had studied under Woodrow Wilson at Johns Hopkins, brought mildly progressive views to the statehouse. He was able to do so because he had the prerequisite for successful political campaigning in Arkansas, an oratorical style modeled on that of William Jennings Bryan and perfected in hundreds of rafter-shaking speeches delivered at high school commencements, church gatherings, and civic functions all across the state. As a Wilsonian ''scholar in politics,'' he was active in the Southern Sociological Congress, describing his role as ''preaching the new crusade of the new chivalry of health and sanity in dealing with every vital problem of civic and social welfare and supplementing the 'pew' religion of the different creeds with the 'do' religion of 20th Century Efficiency.'' [6] Brough's progressivism went down with Woodrow Wilson's in the national relapse into normalcy.

When Alexander Heard came to Arkansas in 1946 to undertake the field studies for V. O. Key's landmark *Southern Politics in State and Nation* he was astonished to find that for thirty years the state's leading newspaper had not endorsed a gubernatorial candidate in the Democratic primary, where the choice was actually made. The *Gazette* stood mute, J. N. Heiskell explained, because these elections had not involved a matter of ''significant public policy'' since the passing of Jeff Davis. Key's chapter on Arkansas is entitled ''Pure One-Party Politics.'' [7]

Some Arkansas politicians who ascended to the national stage

5. Robert A. Leflar, *The First Hundred Years: Centennial History of the University of Arkansas* (Fayetteville: University of Arkansas Foundation, 1972), p. 74.

6. Leland Duvall, *Arkansas: Colony and State* (Little Rock: Rose Publishing Co., 1973), pp. 7, 8.

7. V. O. Key, Jr., *Southern Politics in State and Nation* (New York: Vintage Books, 1949), p. 183.

took on ideological coloration from the issues of the day, as in the case of Joe T. Robinson, vice-presidential candidate on the Democratic ticket with Al Smith, and Senate majority leader for Franklin D. Roosevelt. But, once in Washington, where they usually stayed a long time, Arkansas's representatives divorced themselves from factional local politics, and the voters, proud of the national recognition that came with seniority, seemed to expect them to rise above the unseemly brawling that centered around the statehouse.

The one-party system permitted a prudent politician to return to Congress election after election with only nominal opposition so long as he used his federal connections to take care of the immediate interests of his key supporters. *Southern Politics* described the system as it functioned in the years before the school integration controversy brought on a new eruption of factionalism. There was not even the vaguest sort of grouping along conservative-progressive lines:

> This does not mean that there are no politicians of liberal leanings (such as Brooks Hays and Bill Fulbright) or of conservative inclinations (such as Ben Laney and John McClellan), or that occasions do not occur when individuals of like policy-disposition act in concert. But . . . there have not developed in Arkansas alignments of political leaders organized to give effective expression to differences in political viewpoint . . . Arkansas exhibits a case of political consensus in exaggerated form. And that consensus comes fundamentally from the fact that conservatives control without serious challenge." [8]

When the social programs of the New Deal reached into the poverty-stricken backcountry of Arkansas in the 1930s they began to make changes in this ideologically inert political mass, bringing a new consciousness to poor whites and disfranchised blacks. But this was an influence that worked around, not through, the one-party political process and had little immediate effect upon it.

A resurgence of the old Populist spirit touched Arkansas in 1932 when Hattie Ophelia Wyatt Caraway, appointed to the

8. Key, *Southern Politics,* p. 185.

United States Senate as the widow of the late Thaddeus, won a full term in her own right through the intervention of Huey Long. The Louisiana Kingfish rolled across the state in a sound truck, in seven days delivering thirty-nine speeches in thirty-one counties, anointing Mrs. Caraway as a disciple of his "share-the-wealth" movement.

The appeal of the Long gospel for depression-ridden Arkansans can be seen in the exhortation of Gerald L. K. Smith, one of the Kingfish's principal outriders, who returned to Arkansas years later to establish a fundamentalist redoubt at Eureka Springs: "Let's pull down those huge piles of gold until there shall be a real job, not a little old sow-belly, black-eyed pea job, but a real spending money, beefsteak and gravy, Chevrolet, Ford in the garage, new suit, Thomas Jefferson, Jesus Christ, red white and blue job for every man!" [9] Among those who went down before the invasion from Louisiana was the Wilsonian reformer, Brough, while the main object of Huey Long's wrath, the incipient New Dealer, Joe T. Robinson, wasn't even running but was singled out because of his law firm's corporate clients, conspicuously including the Arkansas Power & Light Company.

The Democratic majority leader's connections with AP&L are often cited as the reason for the selection of the Tennessee Valley, rather than the more suitable area defined by the Arkansas River, for the great New Deal multipurpose development scheme called TVA. "I could have been born in no better place than Arkansas to see first-hand what an electric power monopoly could do to the people," wrote Clyde T. Ellis, who in 1938 ran a successful race for Congress in the northwest district by attacking Senator Robinson's role as the power company's general counsel. [10] Ellis went on to head the National Rural Electric Cooperative Association, and his influence helped make AP&L's heavy-handed political involvement a continuing issue. Still, it was Key's finding that the succession of essentially conservative governors continued unbroken across the New Deal years, with only one, Carl Bailey, distinguishing himself "by

9. T. Harry Williams, *Huey Long* (New York: Alfred A. Knopf, 1971), p. 700.
10. Clyde T. Ellis, *A Giant Step* (New York: Random House, 1966), p. 29.

suspecting that anything was wrong with Arkansas and that something could be done about it." [11]

The pattern held until 1948, when a surge of political activity by returning war veterans brought to the front a handsome Marine colonel, Sidney Sanders McMath. McMath won widespread publicity with a crusading campaign for prosecuting attorney in his home town, declaring political war on Hot Springs's entrenched Mayor Leo McLaughlin, who for many years had run the resort town's local government with protection money openly collected from gambling establishments, brothels, and saloons allowed to flourish in defiance of Arkansas's bluenose statutes.

In general terms McMath talked progressive politics, and his later career would demonstrate his sincerity, but he drew no issues in his gubernatorial campaign more tangible than a demand for "clean government" and the promise of an expanded highway program—items no candidate was likely to come out against. With the help of vigorous leadership from veterans who formed an impromptu "GI" movement in key counties, McMath won a narrow victory over three opponents cast in the familiar Arkansas mold.

If McMath's election could be called a victory for reform it extended no further, as Key noted, than arousing support for common honesty in elections: "In a number of Arkansas communities this is, of course, the fundamental issue, for without free and honest elections the entire democratic process fails. In these communities free and honest elections would be radical, or revolutionary, for an honest count would overthrow the established order." [12]

The established order was in for a good many shocks in the coming decade, but these would derive from forces not yet visible behind the colorful facade of Arkansas's one-party politics.

11. Key, *Southern Politics*, p. 185.
12. Key, *Southern Politics*, p. 201.

14

The Faubus Era

$\mathcal{T}$HERE was a sense of generational change as the GI movement crested and ebbed in Arkansas. Sid McMath brought a vigorous personal style to his administration that tended to alarm the conservative interests, particularly AP&L. He stood with Harry Truman in the successful effort of regular Democrats to turn back the "Dixiecrat" third party launched by his predecessor, Ben Laney, who joined Gov. Strom Thurmond of South Carolina in the effort to exploit racist feelings aroused in the South by Truman's mild civil rights program. Nationally this made McMath a glamorous "New South" symbol, and his warm personal relationship with a sitting president gave him prestige at home.

McMath won his second term handily, but when he tried for a third the conservative opposition rallied to defeat him on the very issue that had brought him to office—clean government. In furtherance of his promise to get back-country Arkansans out of the mud, he sponsored a major bond issue to match federal highway construction funds, but he had made no effective change in the system under which the highway commission and key legislators used road funds for political patronage and personal gain. The anti-McMath faction in the general assembly pushed through a special highway audit that turned up enough evidence of waste, fraud, and favoritism to insure the election of a prematurely white-haired symbol of rectitude, Chancellor Francis Cherry of Jonesboro.

The conservative Cherry's tenure in the statehouse was abruptly terminated by one of the discredited highway commissioners, Orval Eugene Faubus. A weekly newspaper proprietor in Madison County who had served with distinction as a National Guard captain in the European theater, Faubus had signed on early with the GI movement and secured a place as an insider in the McMath administration. Few political leaders took him seriously when he entered the race against Cherry, who was believed to be assured a second term. Faubus, however, was endowed with the natural equipment for a Jeff Davis–style campaign, and an opponent who was uniquely vulnerable to it. Voters in the mountain counties rallied to the self-styled "hillbilly from Greasy Creek" in numbers sufficient to put him into the runoff.

The Cherry forces panicked and tried to hang a Communist label on Faubus based on his brief attendance at a radical self-help academy, Commonwealth College, and his outspoken father Sam's proud self-identification as an unreconstructed Eugene V. Debs socialist. The *Gazette,* which was tacitly supporting the lackluster Cherry on the ground that there was no good reason to turn him out, denounced this McCarthy-style smear in a front-page editorial, and liberals in the McMath camp, including key black leaders, rallied behind Faubus.

Numan V. Bartley and Hugh D. Graham, who in the seventies set out to update V. O. Key's earlier survey of *Southern Politics,* summarized Faubus's first term as the successful effort of a capable politician to balance competing interests and strengthen his ties with county leaders. He catered to rural voters through increased state support for public education and higher old-age pensions, while he propitiated business interests with various favors, including controversial rate increases for the Arkansas-Louisiana Gas Company, whose colorful president, Witt Stephens, remained a powerful influence throughout the Faubus era. The number of welfare recipients was drastically reduced, an action that hit poor blacks hardest, and the governor supported legislation designed to forestall public school desegregation; at the same time black undergraduates were admitted to the University of Arkansas and Faubus made room for a half-dozen blacks on the State Democratic Central

Committee. Bartley and Graham concluded: "By the time of the 1956 primary elections, Faubus had covered all flanks." [1]

In hindsight, there is splendid irony in Faubus's 1956 campaign. The United States Supreme Court had rendered its *Brown* decision outlawing segregation in the public schools and, although the lower courts had not yet begun implementing the new ruling, the resistance movement was forming across the South. Arkansas's usual tolerance in racial matters had been put to the test by the rise of local White Citizens Councils passionately calling for last-ditch defiance, and their leader, James D. Johnson, was the governor's principal challenger. A stump speaker who specialized in oratorical close combat, Johnson directed the full blast of segregationist invective at Faubus—but the ultimate effect was to alarm white conservatives and solidify the black vote. Upper-income urban precincts that had gone 90 percent against Faubus in 1954 gave him 60 percent of their votes against Johnson, while his hill country support held firm.

By 1958, when Faubus made his third-term bid, the desegregation controversy had sharpened to the point where he could no longer take refuge in the kind of circumlocution that had enabled him vaguely to identify himself as the economically progressive candidate in his first race, and in the second appear "still as vaguely as he could manage, the moderate candidate." [2] In the fall of 1957 he confronted the prospect of desegregation on his very doorstep; Little Rock's Central High School was scheduled to open with a few carefully screened black students among its more than two thousand whites.

As far back as 1954 the Little Rock School Board had announced a policy of voluntary compliance with the new Supreme Court ruling. A limited, phased plan to desegregate the schools from the top down was hammered out by school officials in collaboration with citizens' groups of both races, and endorsed by the federal district court when the National Association for the Advancement of Colored People attacked it as

---

1. Numan V. Bartley and Hugh D. Graham, *Southern Politics and the Second Reconstruction* (Baltimore: Johns Hopkins University Press, 1975), pp. 54, 55.

2. Bartley and Graham, *Southern Politics and the Second Reconstruction,* p. 54.

tokenism. The plan had the solid, if reluctant, support of the city's dominant business community, which regarded this minimal compliance as preferable to the dislocations that predictably would follow in the wake of overt defiance of the federal courts.

Faubus, however, was under intense pressure from the Citizens Councils, political leaders in the plantation belt, and segregationist southern governors led by Marvin Griffin of Georgia. They urged upon him the doctrine of "interposition," a dubious exhumation of extreme states' rights theory most legal scholars had assumed was disposed of by the Civil War. The contention was that a sovereign state was entitled to interpose its police powers to preserve order when the actions of the federal government threatened to disturb the tranquility of a local community.

Failing in private efforts to persuade the Little Rock School Board to initiate delaying action in state court, the governor elected for the first time to move out in front himself. Three days before the scheduled school opening he made a dramatic appearance in chancery court to support an appeal for an injunction brought by the segregationist Mothers League of Little Rock. Faubus testified that he had unspecified information that there would be violence if black students showed up at Central High School.

The following day Ronald N. Davies, a North Dakota federal district judge temporarily sitting in the Arkansas jurisdiction, ordered the school board to ignore the chancery court injunction and proceed with its desegregation plan, enjoining "all persons in any manner, directly or indirectly" from interfering therewith. Two days later Faubus ordered the Arkansas National Guard to seize Central High School because of "evidence of disorder and threats of disorder." [3] Judge Davies on September 4 countered with an order for admission of the black students, and on September 5 they were turned back by Faubus's troops.

Whether he intended it or not, Orval Faubus had now precipitated a confrontation of historic dimensions. The scores of national correspondents who flocked to Little Rock found no evidence to sustain the governor's still-undocumented claim of impending violence, and Mayor Woodrow Mann branded it a

3. *Arkansas Gazette*, Sept. 3, 1957.

hoax in a telegram to President Eisenhower. Faubus's reply was a telegram asking the president to "stop unwarranted interference of federal agents," and on September 8 he went on national television to reaffirm his role as "preservator of the peace." [4]

President Eisenhower summoned Faubus to the vacation White House at Newport, Rhode Island, on September 14, a move that precipitated a great scurrying behind the scenes as various honest brokers, including Congressman Brooks Hays of the Little Rock district and a committee of southern governors, sought to work out a face-saving compromise. Nothing came of this, and on September 20 Judge Davies held that the National Guard was not being used to preserve law and order, and specifically enjoined Faubus from further interference. That evening the state troops were withdrawn.

The following morning some semblance of the mob Faubus had predicted finally turned up at Central High, most of its members coming from out of the city and some from out of the state. There were enough hyperactivists among the thousand persons on hand to test the thin cordon put up by the dispirited Little Rock police, and shortly before noon the city authorities capitulated and removed the black students from the high school. President Eisenhower denounced the mob action as intolerable, and ordered a detachment of 1,100 officers and men of the 101st Airborne Division flown to Little Rock. On September 25 nine black students were back in class, and federal troops occupied positions on the school grounds they would maintain without serious incident for the remainder of the school year.

These events, and those that followed over the next two years, were the subject of millions of printed words and hundreds of hours of network television coverage that made Little Rock a worldwide symbol of racist resistance to the accelerating national movement to secure the black minority's civil rights. Fixed in the memory of most Americans is the impression of a city beset by rioting and occupied by military force; in

4. *Arkansas Gazette,* Sept. 9, 1957.

fact no single life was lost, no one was injured sufficiently to require hospitalization, and most of the blood that flowed was shed by newspaper and television photographers whose cameras threatened to identify members of the mob.

There was, of course, a great deal of psychic damage, and the potential for physical violence was real enough to require extraordinary courage on the part of the black children who came to fame as the Little Rock Nine, and their constant shepherd, the indomitable Daisy Bates of the NAACP. For the community at large there was a considerable loss of pride, and of educational substance in the following year when the governor pushed through state laws that enabled him to close Little Rock's high schools while he made a foredoomed effort to use public resources to establish a system of segregated "private" schools.

Faubus was the immediate winner; he probably could not have been elected to a third term without the desegregation controversy, while the great emotional charge provided by his defiance of those he identified as meddling outsiders enabled him to remain in office for another eight years. The few politicians who tried to head off his last-minute intervention could be counted among the immediate losers—notably Brooks Hays, who was turned out of the congressional seat he had held for fourteen years by a Faubus-backed segregationist, Dale Alford; and Sid McMath, whose outspokenly indignant reaction very likely foreclosed a promising political career. The worst mistake he made as governor, McMath wryly observed, was building the first paved road in Madison County and letting Orval Faubus out.

For those in the business community, the *Arkansas Gazette* provided a sobering example of the financial penalties that could attend open opposition to the governor: with Faubus's encouragement the Citizens Councils launched a boycott against the newspaper that cut its circulation by 18 percent and cost its owners more than a million dollars in net income. This was a double-edged campaign that reduced the morning paper's long-standing lead over its afternoon competitor, the *Arkansas Democrat,* which had backed the school desegregation plan but now attracted defecting *Gazette* subscribers as it tacitly supported Faubus.

For the time being Orval Faubus had restored the political formula of the Jeff Davis era, resurrecting the traditional symbols that aroused the defensiveness of back-country Arkansans—the city folk, the *Gazette,* meddling Yankee outsiders—in the process unleashing popular passions that cowed most of those who privately questioned the course of dead-end resistance. Invocation of the old shibboleths of white supremacy, touched up by dark hints of Communist conspiracy, served to divert attention from the ultimate futility of his stand against the federal government.

There are literally volumes of speculation as to Faubus's motivation, including the more-or-less self-serving accounts written by several participants in the Central High School showdown. His own explanation remains the one he offered at the time, when he treated the stirring events he precipitated as though they took place in a vacuum. Although Charlotte, Nashville, Louisville, and most of the other major cities of the upper South had responded to the *Brown* decision as did Little Rock, and school districts all across the region were beginning to desegregate under federal court order, Faubus insisted that an unspecified national conspiracy had singled out his state for punitive imposition of an unconstitutional court decree. In support of that view he espoused a legal theory he has not modified in the light of almost a generation of litigation. In 1976, in an oral history recording at the University of Arkansas, Faubus blandly explained to an incredulous Brooks Hays that the *Brown* decision had no legal force and effect in Little Rock in 1957. The requirement for desegregation "was only a law of the case at that time," he said. "It became the law of the land when Congress enacted the Civil Rights law under President Johnson." [5]

Many of Faubus's supporters accepted him as a racist ideologue, and he was usually so portrayed in the national media, but few of his antagonists in Arkansas ever did. The *Gazette* contended from the outset that he had no real concern with racial matters, one way or the other, but was exploiting the

5. Conversation, Orval Faubus and Brooks Hays, June 4, 1976, Oral History Project, University of Arkansas Library, Fayetteville. Used with permission.

highly charged school desegregation issue to maintain himself in power. Jim Johnson, who spoke for the segregationist true believers, always regarded him as suspect. Robert Sherrill, writing of Faubus at the end of his twelve years in office, titled his biographical sketch "How to Create a Successful Disaster," and concluded that Faubus's career had been characterized by "galvanic groping": "There is in Faubus' makeup a weakness that, in moments of pressure, makes him act seldom from logic, often from fear, and even more often from whatever the last stress happens to be before action is demanded of him." [6]

The man who knew Orval Faubus longest was convinced that he was untouched by simple race prejudice. Old Sam Faubus, the self-educated hill farmer who never abandoned the populist faith nor apologized for the radical views that got him arrested for sedition when he protested United States entry into World War I, refused to grant interviews to the journalists who sought him out in Madison County after his son became a national figure in the course of the Little Rock crisis. But, while he would not publicly condemn his flesh and blood, he could not keep his disapproval of the governor's actions wholly to himself; through the years before his death in 1966 he dispatched sharply critical comments to the letters column of the *Gazette* under the pen name Jimmy Higgins.

Orval, Sam Faubus recalled, had never even seen a black until he was grown and went off to Missouri to pick strawberries, and he knew of nothing that had happened since to cause him to reject his father's teaching that racial equality was essential to progress as well as to justice. His son went off the track, Sam Faubus thought, because he never could stand to be looked down on, and Orval believed that the leading citizens of Little Rock had done just that when he confounded them by displacing Francis Cherry in the governor's mansion. This personal resentment reinforced his suspicion that the Little Rock school desegregation plan was deliberately designed to discriminate against poor whites, requiring those in the downtown area to mingle their children with blacks, while the schools in the upper-

---

6. Robert Sherrill, *Gothic Politics in the Deep South* (New York: Grossman, 1968), pp. 84, 85.

income precincts of Pulaski Heights would remain segregated under prevailing residential patterns.

That interpretation is shared by Faubus's principal black antagonist, Daisy Bates. "I could see what was happening to Orval after he got in office," she said. "The white liberals thought he was a political accident and wouldn't be there long, and they had little to do with him. When he put those troops around Central High it was the people in Pulaski Heights he was really trying to get at. I told the liberals then: You all may deserve Orval Faubus, but by God I don't." [7]

The frantic legal and military maneuvering of the early days of the Central High controversy, with its accompanying wave of disorienting publicity, gave way to a sullen stalemate, and the conservative establishment began to pull itself together. Faubus swept the state in his third-term race, but his extremist campaign brought out Francis Cherry and "Business Ben" Laney to join Sid McMath in open opposition. When he closed the high schools the current matriarch of the Fletcher family, Mrs. Adolphine Terry, Vassar '02, who had marched in every progressive cause from the suffragette movement forward, summoned the matrons of Pulaski Heights to the old Albert Pike mansion where she lived all her long life. Out of this came the Women's Emergency Committee to Open our Schools, headed by Vivion Brewer, Smith '21, which would gain increasing influence in a series of special elections that turned back the segregationist effort to take over the Little Rock School Board.

The chamber of commerce moved gradually, and with some trepidation, toward support of reopening the schools in compliance with federal court directives, which by now had been ratified by a unanimous vote of the U.S. Supreme Court. In May 1959 candidates committed to resuming the desegregation program made a clean sweep in the school board election, defeating a slate the governor had backed in a television campaign in which he inveighed against the "Cadillac Brigade." The federal troops were gone now, but when the segregationists tried to rally another street mob a tough new chief of police, Eugene

---

7. Interview with the author.

Smith, left no doubt that he and his men were prepared to maintain order.

If the race issue provided the catalyst for this continuing political struggle, it had now quite clearly devolved into a matter of caste. Bartley and Graham cited the "sharp class cleavages provoked by Faubus' candidacy" as the source of a new coalition that cut across ordinary liberal-conservative alignment, joining together the country club set with militant, upward-striving blacks:

> The poor whites followed Faubus, and the affluent whites,
> concerned about adverse publicity and the closure of the public high
> schools in Little Rock . . . opposed him. Blacks, not surprisingly,
> joined the affluent whites in the anti-Faubus coalition. In the
> countryside the mountain counties that had originally provided the
> governor's voter base continued to support him, but, after the Little
> Rock crisis, they were figuratively elbowed aside by the stampede
> of lowland counties into the Faubus camp.[8]

In subsequent elections Faubus's margins over a variety of candidates, including McMath, were too substantial to leave any doubt that he retained majority support statewide, but there was reason to suspect that some of the old county machines, after having been slowed by the GI campaign, were running again in high gear. In the 1964 election, when Faubus received 60 percent of the vote, Prof. Richard Yates of Hendrix College noted that "the customary top-heavy majorities were returned by the three most faithful counties: Crittenden, 93 per cent; Newton, 96 per cent; and Madison, ever striving for perfection 99 per cent."[9] Crittenden, in the Mississippi Delta, had been the site of the GI movement's most spectacular campaign to clean up long-standing voting irregularities, and Newton and Madison are adjoining "kept" counties in the Ozarks. In a later election, the home folk in Madison outdid themselves, returning a majority for their favorite son that amounted to 104 percent of the registered voters.

Yet in the eight years after the Central High showdown, when

8. Bartley and Graham, *Southern Politics and the Second Reconstruction,* pp. 56, 57.

9. Richard Yates, *The Changing Politics of the South,* ed. William C. Havard (Baton Rouge: Louisiana State University Press, 1973), p. 275.

Faubus's domination of the state government was virtually complete, the basic trends were running directly counter to the election returns. The process of desegregation in the schools, in employment, and in places of public accommodation moved forward in Arkansas about as it did in those upper southern states where the moderates had prevailed. By the time he came to his last term Faubus seemed to have accepted the end of the rigid forms of legal segregation, and even to have welcomed the change.

In his sixth inaugural address in 1965 he made his biennial claim of having provided the greatest improvement in public services in the state's history, and in time-honored fashion advised freshmen legislators how to attract the attention of the *Arkansas Gazette:* "Some day, if you should choose to condemn me because my eyes are brown and my nose is crooked, or because I am from Greasy Creek, you will be reported as showing great independence." Then he went on to the heart of his message: "Most if not all of the improvements in American life sought by the Johnson program are needed by the people of Arkansas." [10]

The program he thus endorsed was the War on Poverty, which embodied an uncompromising commitment to advancing the cause of the black minority on all fronts, and had been presented to Congress at a televised joint session which saw Lyndon Johnson intoning the marching song of the civil rights movement: "We Shall Overcome."

When Orval Faubus finally vacated the governor's office in 1968, Jim Johnson stepped down from the state supreme court bench and offered himself as a replacement. Slashing at his opponents in his usual fashion, "Justice Jim" led a crowded field that included the moderate Brooks Hays to win the Democratic nomination with 52 percent of the vote. Then, in the general election, came the biggest upset in a century—the election of the most uncommon of Arkansans, Winthrop Rockefeller, a Republican mountaineer who owned his own mountain.

10. John L. Ward, *Readings in Arkansas Government,* ed. Walter Nunn (Little Rock: Rose Publishing Company, 1973), p. 146.

In response to Johnson's blatantly racist campaign the coalition that had formed in opposition to Faubus pushed past the break-even point, delivering 54 percent of the vote to the multimillionaire whose family held title to the progressive wing of the GOP. Rockefeller swept the cities and towns, running up totals of nearly 80 percent in the black and upper-income white precincts of Little Rock, while Johnson registered slender majorities only among lower-income whites. Years of Faubus's one-man rule had left the Democratic organization a shambles, and Rockefeller's sweep gave the Republicans the lieutenant governor's office and the congressional seat in the northwest district.

Aside from its ideological overtones, the election was a demonstration of how far urbanization had advanced in once-rural Arkansas. And it showed too that blacks, coming into their own under the protection of the federal courts, had achieved real weight in statewide politics: two years before, when Rockefeller ran against Faubus, they had been put off by his Republican label and his refusal to make an unconditional endorsement of the federal civil rights bill, and Rockefeller had lost; this time around they turned out in force and provided his margin of victory.

Winthrop Rockefeller came to the governor's office unburdened by the usual political baggage, and endowed with personal financial and organizational resources unknown to any other governor in the history of the Republic, except his brother Nelson, who presided over the statehouse at Albany. He had gained acceptance as a useful, if remote, citizen in the thirteen years since he founded a luxurious cattle-breeding ranch atop Petit Jean Mountain and settled down there to make a new life for himself. He was an effective chairman of the Arkansas Industrial Development Commission, using his own funds to bring in top-flight staff members, and his connections with the Rockefeller Brothers and Chase Manhattan to convince expanding industries that Arkansas was a good place to locate a plant. A huge bear of a man who affected a western-style Stetson and high-heeled boots, he had been welcomed warmly by his adopted fellow citizens when he went among them as a nonpolitical apostle of progress.

All that changed when he came to the statehouse. There he encountered head-on the Arkansas legislature, traditionally the kept preserve of special interests, and, perhaps because of an unadmitted sense of guilt, a citadel of near-paranoid parochialism. John L. Ward, editor of the *Conway Log Cabin-Democrat,* who served as Rockefeller's campaign director, saw the new governor recoil before the "personal ridicule and derision" that greeted him: "At first he was bewildered by the partisanship and by their behavior so in contrast to his own fair-minded and genteel up-bringing." [11] But the big man also had been a well-decorated infantry officer in the Pacific during World War II, and four weeks into the legislative session he went upstairs to the house chamber to take up the challenge:

> A few men have attempted to choke off the development of better
> government in Arkansas . . . to embarrass the new state
> government in every way possible. . . . They have attempted to
> show, at any cost, that a Republican governor cannot possibly
> accomplish anything with a legislature made up almost entirely of
> Democrats. . . . I must tell you now—in the most emphatic
> terms—that I will not sit quietly in the governor's office while a few
> legislators do their best to dismantle the executive branch of
> government. [12]

The feud was to continue through Rockefeller's two terms. His personal habits, including his fondness for the bottle, became an issue. "Politicians drink in Arkansas . . . like fish some of them, but they never publicly admit it," Ward wrote. "Rockefeller never was much of a politician. He couldn't remember when to say nothing or lie." [13] But by main strength and stubbornness he pushed through programs conventional politicians gave only lip service—prison reform, improvement of health and welfare programs, reorganization of state bureaus long mired in patronage. He met his obligations to his black supporters with precedent-breaking appointments in the state government. Frequently at his own expense, he brought in the best experts he could find to assess Arkansas's needs, and trans-

11. John L. Ward, *Readings in Arkansas Government,* p. 164.
12. Ward, *Readings in Arkansas Government,* p. 163.
13. Ward, *Readings in Arkansas Government,* p. 164.

lated their recommendations into programs he proposed to finance through increased taxes and new bond issues. "The question before us," he told the legislature, "is whether to leave these needs alone, and allow them to become the permanent character of Arkansas, or to meet them head-on, and enjoy growth such as we have never seen before." [14]

He did not always or even usually prevail. At one point he was funding his new department of human resources out of his own capacious pocket because the recalcitrant legislature had cut off its appropriations. And when he decided to try for a third term—prompted, Ward thought, by knowledge that Orval Faubus was preparing to come down from the hills and run again—he must have had some intimation of the cancer that was soon to ravage his huge frame. In his farewell address to the legislature he said:

> It has been said by some that I asked for too much. Perhaps so. You tell me—what quality of leadership would ask too little? What sort of leadership would be content merely to maintain a standard of living that for so long has been so meager for so many? The shame upon me and my administration would have been in not struggling for something better. Today I am not ashamed. . . . The most meaningful measurement of progress is that certain things are no longer acceptable to us as a people. [15]

The election in which he was defeated demonstrated that Rockefeller's regime marked a transition as significant as any in Arkansas's history, not merely in its considerable programmatic accomplishment, but in the changing public attitudes it fostered and confirmed. In the election of 1970 Faubus, "sporting a new mod haircut, a new thirty-one-year-old wife, a slimmed-down profile, and a network of courthouse loyalties," [16] managed to lead a big field in the first Democratic primary, but he only attracted 37.3 percent of the total vote. In the runoff he was devastated by Dale Bumpers, a bright young political unknown from the small hill town of Charleston, who was clearly the representative of a new generation with a new point of view.

14. Ward, *Readings in Arkansas Government*, p. 166.
15. Ward, *Readings in Arkansas Government*, p. 167.
16. Bartley and Graham, *Southern Politics and the Second Reconstruction*, p. 147.

Bumpers simply ignored Faubus's Jeff Davis–style diatribe against him and swept every section of the state except the plantation belt. In his inaugural address he took up where Rockefeller's farewell address left off: "We must not waste the new awakening of our people." [17]

Toward the end of his first term in office, in which he sponsored many of the reforms for which Rockefeller's experts had done the groundwork, Bumpers was described by Ed Stanfield, a discerning and not uncritical Arkansas political writer: "Dale Bumpers is a moderate in all things, including his assessment of himself and his accomplishments, and the changes occurring in the state. He is moderate both by natural disposition and by design, for he believes that moderation is what Arkansas most wants and needs at this point in its history." [18] That description applied to most of the bright, urbane young men who moved into the places of political power with the close of the Faubus era.

17. Ed Stanfield, *South Today* 3 (May 1972), p. 3.
18. Stanfield, *South Today,* p. 5.

15

The Forces of Change

$\mathcal{S}$OME years ago professional boosters designated Arkansas "The Wonder State" and began to promote its attractions as "The Land of Opportunity." To that end a scenario was developed that sought to demonstrate that within its boundaries could be found all the natural resources required to sustain a modern civilization—fertile land, benign climate, abundant water, ferrous and nonferrous minerals, oil and gas—if only they could be properly exploited. If this perhaps strained the facts, it also reflected the extraordinary psychological isolationism that has colored the relationship of Arkansans with the outside world. In part a product of the inherited trauma of a lost war and its aftermath, the attitude is somewhat different from the defensive parochialism that characterized all the Confederate states for a century after Reconstruction. The reason may be that the frontier did in fact survive in Arkansas long after the main body of settlers had pushed on across the great plains.

E. E. Dale, chairman of the history department of the University of Oklahoma, thought the pre-existence of his state as a federal preserve had a great deal to do with it. "Of all the states lying immediately west of the Mississippi River," he wrote,

Arkansas alone found further westward advance of its citizens stopped at its western border by the Indian Territory. . . . Yet the human tide of settlers continued to advance and press against this immovable barrier until virtually every acre of arable land in the

162

western half of the state was occupied as had been that in the
eastern half long before. What took place was what occurs when a
broad, sluggish stream has had thrown across it a dam rising higher
than the river's banks. Gradually the water rises until it forms a
broad deep millpond behind the dam.[1]

Adjacent to the "millpond" the hell-roaring past merged un-
abated into the present. "There is no Sunday west of St.
Louis," the saying went, "and no God west of Fort Smith." [2]
The territory provided a sanctuary for desperadoes of all descriptions, and many of these became familiars, and sometimes
heroes, to the farmers who filled in the valleys and clung to the
slopes of the Ozarks and Ouachitas. The remnants of Quantrill's
raiders rode through those parts, followed by Jesse and Frank
James, the Youngers, Belle Starr, and the Dalton boys.

Such law and order as might exist west of Fort Smith depended in large part on the man assigned there as federal district
judge. He presided over a court unique in the federal system,
for in criminal cases originating in Indian Territory it had first
and final jurisdiction; there was no appeal from its verdict except to the president for pardon or commutation. When Judge
Isaac Charles Parker arrived in 1875 by appointment of President Grant eighteen prisoners charged with murder awaited his
attention. He cleared the docket in short order; fifteen were convicted, eight sentenced to hang, and one was shot while trying
to escape. Six went together to the gallows outside the old army
headquarters, where Arkansans turned out by the thousands to
watch retribution being exacted. This first issue of Judge Parker's court attested that he had an even hand so far as racial discrimination was concerned; the noose went around the necks of
three whites, two Indians, and one black.

In his twenty-one years on the bench Judge Parker sentenced
160 men to death and saw seventy-nine hang. This was by no
means a one-sided proposition; a like number of the United
States marshals who rode into Indian Territory as agents of his
court bit the dust. Defending his frequent choice of something

1. E. E. Dale, "Arkansas: The Myth and the State," *Arkansas Historical Quarterly*
12 (Spring 1953): 20.

2. Glenn Shirley, *Law West of Fort Smith* (Lincoln: University of Nebraska Press,
1968), p. 29.

less than law-abiding citizens for this duty, the judge conceded that a coward might very well be a highly moral man, but asserted that "he could not serve as a marshal in the Indian country." [3] Three generations later Arkansans were still prepared to take to their hearts a fictional prototype of Judge Parker's gunslingers, Marshal Rooster Cogburn, who emerged in Charles Portis's novel *True Grit* to ride across the motion picture screen bearing the lineaments of John Wayne.

While the frontier spirit lived past its time in the western reaches of the state, another anachronism held the rest of Arkansas in thrall. The plantation system, with its year-in, year-out struggle for survival for all it embraced, from landowner to renter to sharecropper, pulled down the general level of prosperity, and militated against the formation of the capital required to diversify the agrarian economy. "Political leaders and small businessmen (there were few others) remained under the spell of the agrarian mystique long after the rest of the country was well underway with the evolution of a high-profit economy," Leland DuVall has written. "The mood of the state was primarily defensive." [4]

Breaks in the pattern were few. Early in the century it was found that rice was ideally suited to the soil, climate, and abundant water resources of the Grand Prairie, and what would become in time a major crop was introduced, primarily by grain farmers of German stock moving down from the Middle West. There was a significant, but hardly a major oil strike at Smackover, near the Louisiana border. Loggers introduced reforestation, encouraging the expansion of woodworking plants that became the largest single employer of industrial labor. Strip mining of bauxite began early in the century, but the ore was shipped out for processing until World War II. Debilitated though the old monarch might be, cotton remained king for the first half of the twentieth century.

The inflation of World War I, when the price of cotton soared

3. Shirley, *Law West of Fort Smith*, p. 59.

4. Leland DuVall, *Arkansas: Colony and State* (Little Rock: Rose Publishing Co., 1973), pp. 3, 4.

to thirty-five cents a pound and temporary military installations turned loose a flood of payroll money, spread comparative prosperity over most of the population. The adventurous ones used the extra cash to join the outmigration of blacks and whites that would continue in recurring waves, but the bonanza ended with the war and those who stayed home had no option but to go back to farming. In the late twenties the price of cotton began the long slide that would take it below the cost of production—to 16.79 cents a pound in 1929, 9.46 in 1930, 5.66 in 1931. In 1932 the New Orleans exchange recorded the lowest price in half a century, 4.95 cents a pound. That same year great floods on the Mississippi and its Arkansas tributaries cut the state's cotton production by one-third, and the disaster was followed by the worst drought on record.

If the depression created severe economic distress over the whole of the nation, it brought on nothing less than a cultural crisis in Arkansas. In January 1931 an event symptomatic of the unraveling social fabric brought three hundred farmers charging into the little town of England in the plantation country south of Little Rock. The Citizens Bank and Trust Company had closed three days before, and on this Saturday morning Red Cross officials ran out of application blanks and stopped issuing provisions to those whose funds had disappeared in the failed institution.

The growing crowd was fed by farm families arriving in cars, on horseback, in buggies, and on foot. Their organizer, a man named Coney, had said, "When we gets to town, we'll ask for food quiet-like, and if they don't give it to us, we'll take it, also quiet-like." The local leaders recognized that these were hardworking citizens who had fallen on evil times, and the merchants of England volunteered enough foodstuff to meet the immediate demand. The uprising subsided when relief followed in the form of highway construction jobs. But Coney made a prophetic observation: "I think three winters like this one would see them organized. I'll tell you that there's sure goin' to be something tearin' loose 'round there someday." [5]

5. Donald Holley, *Uncle Sam's Farmers* (Urbana: University of Illinois Press, 1975), pp. 3, 4.

Aside from its importance as a portent, the incident at England had significance as a national media event. Accounts in newspapers around the country prompted Will Rogers to quip: "Paul Revere just woke up Concord; these birds woke up America." [6] This in itself was a departure for back-country Arkansans; for generations what they knew of the outside world had reached them word of mouth through their own leaders, or was filtered through the local press, and such word of their plight as reached the outside passed in reverse through the same channels. Now radio was beginning to provide a rudimentary national communications system that reached directly from source to recipient, and the ubiquitous automobile sent reporters ranging far beyond the rail lines. When the desperate farmers of Arkansas did begin to organize they attracted the attention of articulate outsiders sympathetic to their cause, as well as those closer to home who viewed with alarm what they perceived, quite correctly, to be the beginning of the end of a quasi-feudal agricultural regime.

Franklin Roosevelt's first approach to the clearly intolerable conditions in the farm belt was the Agricultural Adjustment Administration, which dealt directly with landowners. The theory was that government payments at this level, coupled with market stabilization, would provide benefits that would trickle down to tenants and renters who stayed on the land, and that work relief projects would take care of those who didn't. But by 1934, Norman Thomas, after a visit to Arkansas's Mississippi Delta country, charged that hundreds of thousands of sharecroppers "are either being driven out on the roads without hope of absorption into industry, or exist without land to cultivate by grace of the landlord in shacks scarcely fit for pigs. No satirist ever penned such an indictment of a cruel and lunatic order of society as was written by the author of the Agricultural Adjustment Act." [7]

While he was in Eastern Arkansas the Socialist leader convinced two of his local adherents, H. L. Mitchell and Henry

6. Holley, *Uncle Sam's Farmers*, p. 4.
7. Holley, *Uncle Sam's Farmers*, p. 83.

Clay East, that what was really needed was a sharecroppers union that could use bargaining power to halt chiseling under AAA contracts. The potential was enormous, for by 1930 63 percent of all Arkansas farmers worked somebody else's land. In July 1934, in a run-down schoolhouse near Tyronza, Mitchell and East brought into being the Southern Tenant Farmers' Union with a membership of eleven whites and seven blacks. Some of the founders were former members of the Ku Klux Klan, and one of the blacks was a survivor of the 1919 massacre of tenants who attempted to organize a protest movement against landlords at nearby Elaine. By the end of 1935 the STFU had its heaviest concentration in northeast Arkansas, but claimed a total of about thirty thousand members scattered across the neighboring states.

It was a hopeless cause from the outset. White tenants were by temperament and tradition unconditioned for co-operative effort, and many were far from ready to accept their idealistic leaders' requirement that they open their locals to blacks on a basis of absolute equality. Blacks had their own oppressive conditioning to overcome. In her memoir of her Arkansas girlhood, Maya Angelou wrote of the agitation that beset her grandmother when her brother failed to return home at nightfall:

> Her apprehension was evident in the hurried movements around the kitchen and in her lonely fearing eyes. The black woman in the South who raises sons, grandsons and nephews had her heartstrings tied to the hanging noose. Any break from routine may herald for them unbearable news. For this reason, Southern blacks until the present generation could be counted among America's arch conservatives.[8]

In their own way, the landlords were as desperate as the tenants. Even with federal aid many were fighting off foreclosure, and great tracts of land had gone under the hammer all over Arkansas. They and their dependents in the little trading centers thought of the plantation system not as a means of making a living but as a way of life, and they were bound to resist anything that threatened the established order, as the STFU

8. Maya Angelou, *I Know Why the Caged Bird Sings* (New York: Bantam Books, 1971), p. 95.

surely did. When Norman Thomas came back to Eastern Arkansas in the spring of 1935 he made a swing through Trumann, Gilmore, Marked Tree, and Lepanto, and then at Birdsong the thin veneer of civility cracked. A group of riding bosses from nearby plantations charged into the meeting where he was about to speak. "Ladies and gentlemen—" began Howard Kester, a union leader, and a voice boomed out, "There ain't no ladies in the audience and there ain't no gentlemen on the platform. We don't need no Gawddamn Yankee bastard to tell us what to do with our niggers." [9] Thomas was dragged off the platform and run out of town.

When he called at the White House to relate his Arkansas experiences to President Roosevelt all Thomas got was an admonition that the STFU must exercise restraint. "I know the South," FDR said, "and there is arising a new generation of leaders in the South and we've got to be patient." [10] It may have been a politician's temporizing answer, but it also was a statement of fact. There was no way the rebellious tenants could bring enough pressure to impose their demands on the system, but there were those in the South who were beginning to accept the fact that the plantation economy would have to change in order to survive.

Failure though it may have been as a continuing union organization, a perceptive student of the period, Donald Holley, in his *Uncle Sam's Farmers* gives STFU credit for touching off the reaction that pushed the New Deal toward far bolder action on the farm front than that undertaken under the discredited AAA. When the union called a cotton choppers' strike that idled 5,000 hands in Eastern Arkansas, a clergyman and a young woman associated with the union were flogged on a lonely country road and the incident made headlines everywhere. Correspondents from all over the world were now traversing the Delta country and most were profoundly shocked by what they saw. "I have traveled over most of Europe and part of Africa," wrote Naomi Mitchinson, an English novelist, "but

---

9. Holley, *Uncle Sam's Farmers,* p. 86.
10. Holley, *Uncle Sam's Farmers,* p. 86.

I have never seen such terrible sights as I saw yesterday among the sharecroppers of Arkansas." The stoop laborers in the fields reminded Frazier Hunt of Chinese coolies he had seen in Manchuria: "They seemed to belong to another land than the America I knew and loved." [11] Jonathan Daniels, bearing a name long honored in the old Confederacy, visited Tyronza and included a scathing denunciation of the tenant system in *A Southerner Discovers the South.*

Arkansans were appalled both by the worsening conditions in the plantation belt and by the bad publicity. In August 1936 Gov. J. Marion Futrell gave up trying to gloss over the press accounts and appointed a group of leading citizens to an Arkansas Tenancy Commission chaired by a man no one could suspect of radical tendencies, Clyde E. Palmer of Texarkana, the tight-fisted publisher of a chain of small dailies in the southern part of the state. Late in 1936 the commission announced its conclusion: "A majority of tenants are unable without assistance to extricate themselves from tenantry. Tenancy has become a serious menace to American institutions, and threatens the fertility of the soil and the character of the people." The report advocated a federal "homestead policy" providing credit at minimal cost to enable tenants to acquire their own farms, and the provision of such services as health care and adult education at public expense. Exaltation of the family farm as a safeguard against subversion was, of course, very much in the conservative American tradition, but it was no less alarming to those in the plantation belt when it was coupled with a demand for legislation to "discourage the ownership of farm lands in large tracts necessitating cultivation through tenancy or day labor." [12]

Most of the recommendations of the Arkansas Tenancy Commission were incorporated in the Bankhead-Jones Farm Tenant Act of 1937. The emergency Resettlement Administration, which had experimented with model communities at Dyess Colony, Lakeview, Plum Bayou, and Lake Dick, was now absorbed into the Department of Agriculture and rechristened the Farm Security Administration. It would, with diminishing suc-

---

11. Holley, *Uncle Sam's Farmers,* p. 92.
12. Holley, *Uncle Sam's Farmers,* pp. 95, 96.

cess, continue to push for new programs of co-operative farming, which the original moving spirit, Rexford G. Tugwell, and
his successor, Will Alexander, correctly foresaw would provide
the only means by which small farmers could stay on the land in
the face of the coming mechanization of agriculture. But this
was the kind of heresy that earned Tugwell the soubriquet "Rex
the Red" in the plantation belt, and was hardly more welcome
to the salvaged tenants, for whom the idea of joint ownership of
land and the means of production had little appeal, even when
accompanied by the unheard-of amenities provided by the
model village at Dyess Colony.

New Deal subsidies did get agriculture back on a paying
basis, and many thousands of black and white Arkansans were
given the boost that permitted them to make the transition to
self-sufficiency. But the very success of these programs in relieving the worst of the human suffering began to erode the per-
missive popular attitudes that had allowed them to come into
being. The old cries of "un-American" began to sound again,
with stultifying effect upon faint-hearted local leaders. The
FSA's national spokesmen preached the necessity of departure
from fee-simple ownership, the hallowed concept of American
agrarians. "The leaders of the agency assumed society, rather
than the individual, was responsible for poverty; but it was the
individual they had to change," Donald Holley wrote. "The
revolutionary potential of the agency lay not in a bogey such as
cooperative farming, but in the attempt to replace traditional attitudes, to teach people things they evidently did not want to
learn or did not know they needed to learn." [13]

The revolution came, but it was made by nonpolitical men—
the engineers in Detroit who perfected a tractor that could do
anything a mule could do, and do it cheaper; the botanists and
entomologists and chemists in the agricultural experiment sta-
tions who found new ways to eliminate the natural enemies of
growing crops, and those in the Agricultural Extension Service
who spread word of these miracles around the countryside; the
soil conservation workers who paid farmers to take unsuitable

13. Holley, *Uncle Sam's Farmers*, p. 175.

land out of row crops, or to terrace it so the topsoil wouldn't run off; the linemen of the rural electric co-operatives who brought energy to replace hand labor in some of the most onerous farm chores; and finally the Rust brothers down at Pine Bluff who contrived an ungainly machine that could pick cotton.

In a single generation these developments combined to change the face of Arkansas. At the beginning of World War II the great majority of Arkansans were still on the land and dependent upon it for a living. By 1975 the average number of workers on Arkansas farms was down to 77,000—58,000 listed as family workers, and 19,000 as hired hands. And the end was not yet in sight; from 1975 to the fall of 1976 the number of farm workers dropped by another 7,000. As the farm population declined the value of farm products rose in inverse ratio; the realized gross income from all farm operations stood at $641.1 million in 1955, passed the billion-dollar mark in 1965, and in 1975 reached $2.24 billion.

The process has eliminated the tenant farmer, at least as he existed in the days of hand labor. Technically speaking, there is still a sharecropper on the old Eagle place down near Lonoke, where the Wheelers once complained that the hands were indentured to the plantation commissary. Allen G. Brummett, whose credentials as an old-timer include a claim to Cherokee ancestry, moved up from Humnoke in 1920 when his father took over as overseer for the family of W. H. Eagle, a brother of the former governor. The land is still owned by Eagle descendants, and "Big Daddy" Brummett is still overseeing it on shares. But there is no trace of the scores of black families who were living there when he arrived; they have been replaced by his sons and two resident workers who are paid an annual wage. Big Daddy meets the payroll and owns the quarter million dollars worth of equipment that makes possible a vastly increased annual yield, in which cotton now usually runs behind soybeans and rice. Stoop labor is a thing of the past; the huge combines that harvest the beans and rice are even equipped with air-conditioned cabs and radios. It is still sharecropping in the sense that Big Daddy divides the returns with the landlord—but these days there is enough on his end to enable him to take off when he feels like it and watch the horses run over at the Oaklawn track.

Big Daddy's operation is modest by current Arkansas standards, a cottage industry compared to the corporate farming of the Delta country where agribusiness flourishes on the scale of the San Joaquin Valley of California.

In 1886 the first Robert E. Lee Wilson arrived from Tennessee to begin cutting timber in Mississippi County, where the New Madrid earthquakes had left a network of swamps, but instead of moving on he prepared the cutover land for cotton production by instituting a drainage system. This brought into cultivation some of the most fabulous agricultural acreage man has yet discovered, with rich black topsoil that reaches an incredible thickness of 1,200 feet, compared to a world average of seven inches. When Robert E. Lee Wilson III came home from Yale in the 1920s the Lee Wilson Company was farming 36,000 acres.

Wilson recalls that his first job was to make a census of the houses that had been clustered around overseers' headquarters as the land went into cotton section by section. Nobody knew how many people lived on the plantation and Wilson is still not sure. He does recall that there were four thousand mules, which meant there were at least two thousand mule drivers; counting women and children, who were also part of the work force, there must have been something on the order of ten thousand people living along the back roads of the Wilson plantation, almost all of them black.

Today the company farms the same acreage with about 300 full-time workers. In the old days almost half the land had to be kept in subsistence crops to feed the mules and the hands, but now all 36,000 acres is devoted to four cash crops—with wheat, rice, and soybeans usually leading cotton. The thousands of houses the young Wilson counted have long since disappeared; the skilled farm machinery operators, whose annual wage puts them in the middle-income range, live, along with workers in the company's related processing enterprises, in the pleasant town of Wilson, where the owning family has created a kind of neo-Williamsburg town square.

Back in the hills beyond the plantation belt the small farmers also have thinned out, but a significant number were able to convert to new forms of production that enable them to make a

living income. On the gentler slopes of the Ozarks and Ouachitas there is good pastureland, and beef and dairy herds have
become commonplace. New mass-production techniques for
poultry and eggs can be employed on any patch farm, and dis-
tributors are available to help finance the operation. In less than
two decades Arkansas moved into first place in the nation in the
production of broilers; in 1975 the cash value of the chicken
crop was $441,889,000, second only to soybeans at
$507,600,000, and well ahead of rice at $322,427,000. Eggs, at
$182,096,000, trailed cotton and cottonseed by only $8,000,000.

The process has spread relative prosperity among all those
who have remained on the land. But these are only the residue
of the far larger number displaced by the agricultural revolution;
in 1960 Arkansas was one of only three states that showed a net
loss of population. Hundreds of thousands of white and black
Arkansans joined the forced migration that began in the depression years and continued for three decades, taking those called
Arkies to California and dumping the others, black and white,
in the inner city ghettoes of the East and Midwest. For many of
these it was a pilgrimage not much less cruel than the Cherokees' trek across the Trail of Tears.

16

Closing the Gap

$\mathcal{S}$INCE the Civil War Arkansas has had a procession of visionary leaders who sought a way to bring into the mainstream of national development a state so well-endowed with natural resources. The populists who approached the problem from the political left, carrying the banner of monetary and antitrust reform, made no headway. Promoters who took their stand on the right did little better as they sought to persuade the national financial community that rich profits would flow from industries processing and fabricating the wealth of raw materials produced in the state.

The dismal legacy of the early public experiments in banking, internal improvement, and railway promotion no doubt had much to do with this. In 1881, when he finally completed liquidation of the long-defunct state banks, W. B. Worthen, founder of Arkansas's leading financial institution, said: "The slow development of this state, due to the disinclination of outside capital to invest here, is in great measure chargeable to the gross mismanagement of these two banking corporations." [1]

This experience left a heavily conservative imprint on the promotional efforts of the state's leaders during the first half of the twentieth century. They were faced with a large, self-renewing surplus of population in relation to job opportunity, and so,

---

1. Works Progress Administration, *Arkansas: A Guide to the State* (New York: Hastings House, 1941), p. 65.

in accordance with the rules of the marketplace, they counted cheap labor among the state's exploitable resources. And, since conservative political dominance was never seriously threatened after Jeff Davis's passing, they could guarantee low taxes and minimal governmental interference to any outside investor who wanted to set up in business in Arkansas.

It was not a situation in which organized labor was likely to thrive. The first union charter was issued in 1865 to typographers of the *Arkansas Gazette* and is still in force. The Knights of Labor took on Jay Gould in 1885, and when there was a flare of violence the state militia intervened on behalf of the railroad. There was a sit-down strike in the mines at Coal Hill in 1886, and by 1898 the United Mine Workers were well established in the Fort Smith area. The Arkansas State Federation of Labor held its first convention in 1904, and that year there was a brief flurry of activity by the radical International Workers of the World in the timber belt of south Arkansas. In 1914 there was another outbreak of violence in the coal fields as the UMW fought against efforts of owners to reimpose the open shop. After two persons were killed and several mines wrecked, the United States District Court intervened, the strikers drove off the federal marshals, and President Woodrow Wilson ordered in the U.S. Cavalry.

In Fort Smith, North Little Rock, where the Missouri Pacific Railway maintained a major repair yard, and in the company towns in the timber belt there were concentrations of union strength. Sporadically, labor and its sympathizers rallied enough support to exert limited political influence. In 1915 the legislature enacted a wages and hours law for women, limiting the work day to nine hours, six days a week, with a minimum wage of one dollar a day for apprentices and a dollar and a quarter for journeymen. Mild as this may seem, the United States Supreme Court in 1925 found it unconstitutional.

Industrial employment grew from 4,500 in 1880 to 26,500 in 1900, but still lagged far behind the growth of the pool of surplus labor. The effect in the marketplace may be seen in the fact that as late as 1938 the average hourly wage was only 28 cents, against 34.8 cents in the southern region as a whole. The only exception to this bottom ranking was in Little Rock, where the wages of skilled labor ran ahead of Memphis, New Orleans, and other comparable southern cities.

In the twenties and thirties Arkansas Power & Light Company assumed the primary burden of industrial promotion, linking it directly to the effort to improve the lot of Arkansans still on the land. The utility's president, Harvey Couch, urged the creation of an indigenous base of purchasing power to feed commercial and industrial growth. In 1926 he proclaimed that electricity could "solve one of the biggest problems confronting the American people—that of making farm life attractive enough and profitable enough to induce young men and women to remain on the farm." [2]

If Arkansas had abundant potential for hydroelectric power, as well as fuel to fire steam generators, there was still the formidable cost of constructing rural lines to serve widely scattered customers. This proved to be beyond the capacity of depression-ridden private enterprisers; by 1935 only 1.2 percent of Arkansas's farms had access to electricity. The rural electrification program, that in forty years would leave less than 1 percent of the state's farms without power, began when New Deal engineers insisted on harnessing the nation's rivers to produce electricity.

In the beginning there was open political warfare between the advocates of public and private power development. AP&L, absorbed into the Middle South holding company, took the lead in the effort to halt the westward march of multipurpose Tennessee Valley Authority–style development, and largely succeeded; although Arkansas's waterways in time were developed by the Corps of Engineers, the central operating authority and related activities of TVA were eliminated. Couch's successor, C. Hamilton Moses, became a leading spokesman in the utility industry's national crusade against "socialized" power, and his spellbinding oratory lifted free enterprise from the realm of economic theory to the level of ideological gospel. This fervor

2. Leland DuVall, *Arkansas: Colony and State* (Little Rock: Rose Publishing Co., 1973), p. 207.

permeated the state and local chambers of commerce, and found an intellectual haven at Harding College in Searcy.

None of this had any direct bearing on, and indeed constituted a diversion from, the state's real economic needs. About the only industrial employers attracted in those years were marginal operators caught in a cost squeeze in the older industrial centers; the notoriously unstable garment industry provided most such refugees, and if a town brought in a plant on the basis of tax exemption, subsidized plant facilities, and official anti-union bias, the increase in employment often did not offset the added expense to the community. Moreover, in the aggregate this kind of hit-or-miss industrialization could not absorb the thousands of workers being forced off the land by new farming techniques, with the result that between 1940 and 1960 Arkansas lost 8.4 percent of its population.

In the bauxite fields the exigencies of World War II produced the beginning of an aluminum processing industry, with both Reynolds Metals and Aluminum Company of America for the first time converting ore into ingots. But the hope that this unique domestic source of bauxite would provide the basis for developing a major fabricating complex came to nothing; high wages and high taxes did not deter the great light metal consumers, the aircraft and space industries, from settling on the West Coast, and the only Arkies who benefitted from end-processing of the metal were those who left home.

The most successful effort to generate new jobs and retain the profits derived from Arkansas's natural products came in the Grand Prairie, where the leading rice farmers managed to develop the means of processing, packaging, and distributing most of their farm product. The result was that the Stuttgart area developed the highest per capita incidence of millionaires to be found in the state. These, mostly endowed with resounding German names, tended to cherish the free-enterprise gospel in its pristine state, despite the fact that their prosperity was built upon a giant co-operative undergirded by government financing and price supports bequeathed by the New Deal.

The producer-owned Riceland Foods complex, made up of twenty-five co-operatives, handled 72,582,864 bushels in 1975, with gross income from sales and services of nearly a half-billion dollars. Riceland's towering elevators received and stored the rice and soybeans the members harvested; some went to market in bulk, but the co-op also processed rice and oil and packaged the product for sale by the major food chains; and finally there was a wholesaling and promotion operation for rice sold under the co-op's own brand name. In recent years more than half the rice and soybean crop has been shipped abroad, usually under government purchase, and Riceland's members found their fortunes entwined with the nation's foreign policy, where their innate conservatism often ran counter to their self-interest. Famine in Bangladesh was good news in Stuttgart, and diplomatic recognition of Communist Cuba was seen as the means of opening a fine new market for rice—a situation that produced new swirls and eddies in the mainstream of Arkansas politics.

The fundamentalist free-enterprise style of industrial promotion began to fade when Orval Faubus persuaded Winthrop Rockefeller to become chairman of the Arkansas Industrial Development Commission. The state agency quickly superseded the utility-dominated effort with a far more sophisticated selling job. Rockefeller imported high-priced development specialists, and used his extensive family connections to attract attention to the state's potentialities. The antilabor leitmotiv necessarily was subordinated, for Faubus had enjoyed almost solid union support and gave it credit for insuring his victory over Francis Cherry. As a practical matter the major companies AIDC began to pursue had never had any illusion that the unions would not follow them South; the most they could expect was an improved bargaining position, and a more appreciative work force developed through their own training. The real lure was the climate and the greatly improved transportation system that placed the industrial corridors intersecting at Little Rock in good position to serve the rapidly expanding "sunbelt" market.

The considerable industrial development of recent years displayed no particular pattern. The Litte Rock Industrial District, which in twenty years built up a 1,000-acre tract on the edge of the city and in 1973 began developing another 1,400 acres, contained almost five million square feet of space devoted to manufacturing, wholesaling, and services. More than ten thousand people were employed there, more than eight thousand in manufacturing enterprises that were wholly new to Arkansas. These factories produced bicycles, rubber goods, highway signs, teletype machines, baked goods, watches, valves, blue jeans, and prefabricated doors. The wholesale distribution served chain and other retail stores over seven states.

By 1976 the hallmarks of the new prosperity were everywhere. In the Ozarks in-migration had made the once-isolated mountain country the fastest-growing rural section in the United States. One welcome result was to double the per capita income in the twenty-two Ozark counties in eight years, but the price had been what many regarded as a shocking change in the area's pastoral beauty and relaxed lifestyle. Aside from the concerns of old traditionalists and young environmentalists there were the practical reservations of planners and public officials faced with an influx that had run to about one-fourth retired and presumably nonproductive persons, and also included a conspicuous number of counterculture colonists who clustered in old resort towns like Eureka Springs. Streams that had always run fresh and clear became polluted and even the most callous chamber of commerce booster must have been offended by the neon-lit strip of franchised vendors that began to blend the once markedly individual towns of Rogers, Springdale, and Fayetteville into a faceless urban complex.

Ginger Shiras, who represented the third generation of a newspaper family rooted in Baxter County, where the rate of growth over fifteen years had been a startling 111 percent, wrote: ". . . there is a bottom line to all this change—deeper than the effects of billboards and shopping centers and more basic than the question of how to provide roads and sewer connections. At the bottom is the question of what will be left of a people long among the most money-poor, isolated and clannish in these homogenous United States, a people rich in tradition, breathtaking surroundings and family and community ties." And she answered her own question when she suggested that few seemed to be willing to trade the pleasures of the affluent present for the rigors of the storied past: "It's hard even to pinpoint what is being lost. Television and cars have sneaked off with some of it and the rest is mostly noted only in its passing." [3]

In the cities and towns the boom had produced the usual mixture of spectacular new construction and suburban sprawl, accompanied by the despoilation of the older, low-rise patterns of downtown shopping districts. This reflected an aggressive promotion-mindedness among the business leadership that contrasted with the caution that long was its most pronounced characteristic. In the years after World War II a discouraged entrepreneur seeking funds to promote the fledgling broiler industry complained that the fusty Little Rock banks would lend money only to those who could prove they didn't need it. By 1976 the three leading institutions occupied tall glass towers that dominated the skyline and advertised the services of financial conglomerates; two were topped by ornate private clubs and the other by an elegant Swiss restaurant; and one maintained a deluxe travel agency for the convenience of the increasing number of Arkansans who had begun to qualify as at least junior members of the international jet set.

Arkansas also had begun to develop entrepreneurs who mix business and politics in the expansive Texas style. Chief among these was Witt Stephens, who acquired control of Arkansas-Louisiana Gas Company and in the post-World War II era eased AP&L out of its inside position in the statehouse. Meanwhile his reclusive brother Jackson built the family bond business into an investment banking firm with assets of $143 million, ranked by *Forbes Magazine* in 1976 as tenth in the nation—just behind First Boston Corporation and Goldman Sachs and ahead of Lehman Brothers and Morgan Stanley. Jack Stephens, an Annapolis classmate of Jimmy Carter and a banking associate of his first budget chief, T. Bert Lance, emerged from his cherished obscurity in the course of the 1976 presidential campaign, a connection that promised to make him even more prominent if deregulation of natural gas added, as *Business Week* estimated, some three hundred million dollars in increased value to Stephens-owned reserves. The Stephens investments in 1976 al-

3. Ginger Shiras, *Arkansas Gazette,* Aug. 22, 1976.

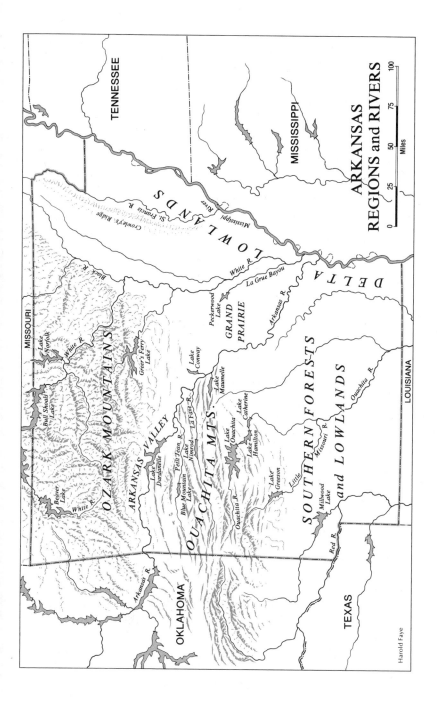

ARKANSAS
REGIONS and RIVERS

Miles
0   25   50   75   100

TENNESSEE

MISSISSIPPI

LOWLANDS

Crowley's Ridge

St. Francis R.

Mississippi River

White R.

DELTA

La Grue Bayou

Peckerwood Lake

GRAND PRAIRIE

Arkansas R.

MISSOURI

Lake Norfolk

White R.

Black R.

Greer's Ferry Lake

Bull Shoals Lake

OZARK MOUNTAINS

Lake Conway

Lake Maumelle

ARKANSAS VALLEY

Lake Dardanelle

Petit Jean R.

Lake Nimrod

La Fave R.

Lake Catherine

Ouachita R.

Lake Ouachita

Lake Hamilton

SOUTHERN FORESTS

Ouachita R.

LOUISIANA

Beaver Lake

White R.

OUACHITA MTS.

Blue Mountain Lake

Ouachita R.

Lake Greeson

Little Missouri R.

Millwood Lake

and LOWLANDS

Arkansas R.

OKLAHOMA

Red R.

TEXAS

Harold Faye

ready were producing income of a million dollars a month for the two brothers.

The great Arkansas River development, the largest civil works project ever undertaken by the United States Corps of Engineers, was completed in the early seventies and began to yield the returns the engineers envisioned when they figured a cost-benefit ratio of 1.5 to 1 on the total investment of $1.2 billion. The river was converted into an artery for water traffic all the way inland to Tulsa, and its course was studded with lakes whose shores could provide sites for new communities. This was expected to contribute significantly to the pattern of development considered ideal by the Economic Development Study Commission appointed by Gov. David Pryor. Noting that almost half the state's population still lived on farms or in towns of less than 2,500, although only a small proportion of these still made their living on the land, the commission urged that this dispersal be maintained so that the urban corridors "will be more like suburbs than central cities. . . . There is no compelling reason for industries and their employees to form congested areas as they locate and settle." [4]

But with all this, the state was still far short of attaining the economic balance and stability its leaders sought. The per capita income rose from 43 percent of the national average in 1929 to 77 percent in 1973, but in 1976 the commission projected a curve that would not bring the average to 90 percent until 1983. In 1974 the median income of $9,229 put more than half of Arkansas families in the low-to-moderate income bracket, while 27 percent were still rated below the poverty line by federal family income standards. In 1977 a new census classification rated 18.5 percent of the population as poor, against a national average of 11.4 percent. Despite the improvement, Arkansas's poverty percentage was still the third highest in the nation—topped only by Mississippi, 26.1, and Louisiana, 19.3.

These economic disparities reflected the fact that Arkansas still had not been able to absorb into productive employment the

4. Report and Recommendations, Arkansas Economic Development Study Commission, Governor's Office of Planning, Little Rock, October 1976.

workers displaced by the rapid mechanization of agriculture. The heritage of the years of racial discrimination consigned a disproportionate number of blacks to the ranks of the un- and underemployed. The results were particularly apparent in northeast Arkansas, where almost a third of the families were below the poverty line. Although the town of Blytheville enjoyed a remarkable industrial boom, the new plants had not yet made room for many of the able-bodied blacks concentrated on its south side. Yet the neighborhood provided a marked contrast to the misery evident there in the depression years when black sharecroppers began drifting in to build shacks on a great sawdust dump. For the most part the houses were painted and improved, the yards were tended, and the black children who played along the streets were unmarked by the telltale signs of malnutrition. Probably less than half of those who lived there were employed full time; the rest managed to subsist, and under the circumstances maintain a remarkable level of human dignity, on welfare payments that trickled down in one form or another from state agencies and the federal government.

There were those in Arkansas, as elsewhere, who considered this situation not only an indefensible violation of the Protestant work ethic, but a dispensation that created more social problems than it resolved. It seemed evident that the flashily dressed young blacks lounging along what were once the prime shopping streets in downtown Little Rock contributed to the rising crime rate; these were men and women passing out of school age without being picked up by the upward mobility that had opened white collar jobs in business and government to the expanding black middle class. At this level Little Rock was as visibly desegregated as any city in the nation, and in almost all respects the lowering of the old barriers seemed to be more advanced than in most cities with no claim to the southern heritage.

There were still traces of racism, but its manifestations were sub rosa for the most part. If there were enclaves in the back country where hard-handed peace officers still felt it their duty to "keep the niggers in their place," the weight of public opinion statewide had shifted against them—and it was not only federal authorities but the state police who rode in to take over at any sign of serious racial tension. Black civil rights lawyers, some of them University of Arkansas graduates, practiced successfully in most of the larger towns. A kind of collective ombudsman, ACORN, the acronym for Arkansas Community Organization for Reform Now, functioned in a fashion that had caused it to be cited by the radical San Francisco magazine, *Mother Jones,* as one of the few effective survivors among the community action groups that emerged from the left-wing youth movement of the sixties. ACORN's often-strident criticism of the system was treated respectfully by the public and private bureaucrats and was widely publicized by the media.

When Central High School opened in the fall of 1976 a front-page article in the *New York Times* bore the headline: "Little Rock School Now Integration Model." The institution that once served as a symbol of racist resistance to desegregation had an able black principal, Morris Holmes, presiding over a student body about evenly divided between the two races, a mixture maintained by bussing in whites from the affluent communities in the expanding western section of the city. "Central is now one of the most effectively desegregated public schools in the United States," the *Times* reported. "No one is able to explain fully how this relaxation came about. . . . Whatever the reasons, much of the community is pleased and proud." [5] The Little Rock Chamber of Commerce claimed credit for the *Times* article as a product of its well-financed national public relations campaign, and clearly regarded the city's newfound reputation for racial harmony as its most valuable asset in the drive for economic growth.

Arkansans had not, of course, been born again purged of all their inherited prejudices, but there had been a significant change in attitude from generation to generation; if there was still some muttering about the rapid upgrading of the black minority's status, there was no one of consequence to stand up in public and argue that the old segregated society could or should be reinstated. The result was to free the leadership of the presumed necessity of maintaining a level of political rhetoric that simply glossed over the economic realities of a traditionally

5. Roy Reed, *New York Times,* Sept. 5, 1976, p. 1.

poverty-ridden state. There could have been no more succinct and realistic an appraisal of Arkansas's condition than that offered in 1974 by Dale Bumpers, when he served as chairman of a human resources committee set up by the Southern Growth Policies Board:

> The technology revolution in agriculture . . . has made manual labor obsolete for millions of Southerners and has made almost impossible the historic self-sufficiency of the small farmer. This same revolution has left millions of people, black and white, in areas where there are no jobs. Despite migration, there is still a surplus of people seeking a livelihood in the rural areas.
>
> . . . .
>
> The system of legal segregation for three centuries specifically discriminated against black Southerners in education, employment and access to housing and other public services. The legacy of this discrimination has still not been overcome.[6]

Governor Bumpers addressed the report to his colleague, Gov. Jimmy Carter of Georgia, who was then chairman of the Growth Policies Board. Both were recognized as leading apostles of the new southern pragmatism that in 1976 made possible the national resurgence of a united Democratic party.

6. Report of Technical Committee on Human Resources and Public Services, Southern Growth Policies Board, Research Triangle Park, North Carolina, November 1, 1974.

Epilogue

$\mathcal{T}$WENTY years ago, when I still lived in Arkansas, I wrote a book called *An Epitaph for Dixie*. My thesis was that, for better or worse, the emerging demography of the New South was bound to alter the distinctive regional values of the Old, rooted as they were in peculiar institutions already in terminal disarray—the agrarian economy, the one-party political system, and legal segregation. "History does not run backward," I concluded, "and it buries its own dead." [1]

In Arkansas the transition that brought on this obituary mood is, by any rational test, complete. The old institutions are altered beyond recognition, and the politicians who tried to maintain them past their time are gone. But Arkansans have a way of confounding both their apologists and their critics, and this is a particular hazard in an appraisal like this one. Enjoined to concentrate on the broad issues that have united—and divided—state and nation, I found myself using *Arkansan* as a generic term—or at best taking into account only the obvious divisions between upcountrymen and flatlanders, or between the ordinary run of black and white citizens and those I have called, in a term borrowed from John Gould Fletcher, the broadcloth gentry. Arkansans are far more various than this suggests; the

---

1. Harry S. Ashmore, *An Epitaph for Dixie* (New York: W. W. Norton & Company, 1957), p. 189.

scholarly works attempting to analyze their behavior reflect a mass of contradictions behind the image as it usually appears in the eye of the outside beholder.

Consider the election of 1968, in which the voters simultaneously gave substantial majorities to the internationalist dove, J. William Fulbright, the integrationist Republican, Winthrop Rockefeller, and the racist hawk, George Wallace. A political scientist I know concluded that this could only be accounted for as a manifestation of abysmal, and quite likely perverse, ignorance. But another, who took a closer look, thought the vote reflected a remarkable sophistication; Arkansans, ordinarily the most loyal of Democrats, not only split but shredded the ticket because they saw all three of these disparate types as mavericks, and, duly considering the other choices available, took the occasion to express their general dissatisfaction with the way things were going at home and abroad. Two years later they rejected Rockefeller, sent Orval Faubus back to Madison County, and elected Dale Bumpers, which must represent about as clear a mandate for a fresh start as any electorate could contrive.

An analyst examining the voting pattern over the last century would have to concede an element of perversity, but I have never thought ignorance had much to do with it. It is true that Arkansas, by national standards, always has been deficient in formal education. In 1852 Gov. John Selden Roane declared, ''I am convinced, after careful investigation into the history of the common school, that no possible good can come if it.'' [2] The governor, however, was defending not ignorance, but the adequacy of the private academies that sprang up everywhere in the state as settlement thickened. If these schools could not be said to have been designed to reach the masses, it is apparent that ambitious children of the backcountry reached them; there is an impressive mastery of language evident in public papers and private correspondence all the way back to the territorial era. And even those whose lack of schooling is reflected in quaint

2. Leland DuVall, *Arkansas: Colony and State* (Little Rock: Rose Publishing Co., 1973), p. 108.

spelling and archaic usage, or the inability to spell at all, often spoke with eloquence and precision that impressed those who took the trouble to hear them out.

There is a strong tradition of self-education, which left an imprint on many who made no claim to scholarly credentials. Letters to the editor of the *Arkansas Gazette* were notable for erudition as well as choler in the days when most originated in small towns or along the rural free delivery routes; I have often been touched by an encounter with a well-spoken elderly subscriber who told me he had learned his letters reading the venerable "Old Lady."

Not long ago, driving out of the Ozark town of Hardy, we came to a place where the highway loops before it crosses the Spring River and the railroad that runs alongside, setting off a gabled Victorian house, most of it falling into ruin, but with smoke rising from the chimney of an ell at the back. We stopped to inquire who lived there, and came upon Carmack Sullivan. The old house, he said, belonged to his family, and its lone occupant was his Aunt Theresa, who declined all entreaties to move out on the ground that she was born there eighty-six years ago and could see no reason to leave now.

The house was built, Sullivan said, by his grandfather, who was worn out after he helped push the railroad across the mountains, and decided to stay on as division superintendent for the Saint Louis & San Francisco. And he recalled that his grandmother had been even more attached to the place than Aunt Theresa. She arranged to have the conductor on the morning train throw off the *New York Times,* and when her grandson stopped in to see her he found her fully informed about the affairs of the great world, but wholly ignorant of the gossip from Hardy, a half-mile down the road, which she no longer bothered to visit, or from Wahpeton Inn within sight across the river, a now-vanished summer watering place for city people. Sullivan remembered that his grandmother was particularly interested in the career of their namesake, John L.

In this century Arkansas has spent a disproportionate share of its scant public funds to create a school system in the prevailing national mode. Separate and unequal though they may have been, these schools taught blacks and whites from the same textbooks; distracted by the obvious inequity, few outsiders have understood the profound implications of this dispensation. If most white Arkansans, as Howard Odum said of southerners in general, did not quite appraise blacks as the same sort of human being they themselves were, they nevertheless saw them always as part of the same society. The long, shared history, and the unadmitted ties of blood, prevented anyone on either side from taking seriously the notion that there might develop here a separate ethnic culture.

"Recently a white woman from Texas, who would quickly describe herself as a liberal, asked me about my home town," Maya Angelou wrote. "When I told her that in Stamps my grandmother owned the only Negro general merchandise store since the turn of the century, she exclaimed, 'Why, you were a debutante!' Ridiculous and even ludicrous. But Negro girls in small Southern towns . . . were given as extensive and irrelevant preparation for adulthood as rich white girls. . . . While white girls learned to waltz and sit gracefully with a tea cup balanced on their knees, we were lagging behind, learning the mid-Victorian virtues with very little money to indulge them." [3] Many, if not most Arkansans came to understand that this was the ultimate, intolerable cruelty—imposing the aspirations of the closed white society on blacks while denying them the means to realize them.

The University of Arkansas was a product of Reconstruction, and a durable myth has it that the institution was tucked away in the inaccessible northwest corner of the state because blacks were few in the Ozarks and the new intellectual citadel could thus preserve Anglo-Saxon purity in defiance of the Yankee conquerors. In fact the university went to Fayetteville because the citizens of the old Whig bastion always had been among the most education-minded in the state, and proved they meant it by putting up more land and cash than any of the other communities that bid for the proposed institution. That, even so, was a minor contribution, for at birth the umbilical cord extended to

3. Maya Angelou, *I Know Why the Caged Bird Sings* (New York: Bantam Books, 1971), p. 87.

Washington, the citadel of the late enemy, which also happened to be the source of federal funds for land-grant colleges.

The founding board of trustees was as remarkable a body as any university could claim; it included an Ohio judge, a Yale Law School graduate who had served as a general in the Union army, a German Jewish immigrant, an Illinois lawyer who had practiced in the office of Lincoln & Herndon at Springfield, and a black who held a doctorate from the University of Ohio and served as Arkansas's superintendent of public instruction. But before one springs to the conclusion that these learned men imposed a liberal imprint upon the institution he runs into the fact that the fellow who actually got it going was the Confederate hero, D. H. Hill, a South Carolinian who obtained his academic credentials at West Point. The general's educational views were reflected in a report to the trustees in which he complained that the faculty was inhibiting growth by stubbornly clinging to a faulty principle "imported from the University of Virginia, namely an exceedingly high standard of scholarship required for graduation." [4]

If the University of Arkansas never managed to achieve first rank among comparable institutions, it nevertheless has had a salutary unifying effect. Its graduates, although comparatively few, constituted an "old boy" network that held together a statewide business and professional community, and its Razorback athletic teams, which often devastated their Texan foes in the Southwest Conference, produced a cult of supporters whose proud hog-calling boosted the spirits of the citizenry at large. That unique role was threatened once the university's jurisdiction was expanded beyond Fayetteville to embrace the former state colleges and a booming commuter campus at Little Rock destined to outstrip the parent institution in enrollment.

In the days when H. L. Mencken inveighed against the hinterland "boobocracy" Arkansas was usually cited as an exemplar of the Bible Belt. It has, certainly, provided a haven for the old-time fundamentalist religion. I have always cherished

4. Robert A. Leflar, *The First Hundred Years: Centennial History of the University of Arkansas* (Fayetteville: University of Arkansas Foundation, 1972), p. 29.

the admonitory banner flung across a downtown Little Rock street by the pastor of a hardshell tabernacle: "A Man Who Doesn't Believe in Hell Won't Be There Five Minutes Before He Changes His Mind." But there was a severe limitation on the ability of the hellfire-and-brimstone preachers to make conversion stick, and I suspect this may have had as much to do with ingrained skepticism as it did with the weakness of the backslid flesh. Brooks Hays, who is surely as civilized a man as ever headed the Southern Baptist Convention, liked to point out that there is something in the atmosphere that has a mind-ventilating effect upon even the most orthodox churchman; he cited as evidence the bishop of the Roman Catholic Arkansas Diocese, Edward Fitzgerald, who cast one of two dissenting votes on the dogma of papal infallibility when the Ecumenial Council convened in Rome in 1871.

The general assembly has displayed a marked proclivity for bizarre applications of the fundamentalist faith. In 1928 Arkansas shared neighboring Tennessee's alarm over the evolutionist heresy, and its anti-monkey statute was the subject of the U.S. Supreme Court's belated 1968 decision declaring unconstitutional state efforts to nullify the scientific theories of Charles Darwin. More recently an occasional member has become exercised over such exotic transgressions as nudism and sodomy, and his fellows have found it expedient to go along, usually after a clownish debate that signified the majority's private recognition that they were dealing in nonsense.

Arkansans have been notorious for drinking wet and voting dry, but they may have been less influenced by moral strictures from the pulpit than by the fact that most families had at least one member who provided firsthand evidence that liquor can create a social problem. J. N. Heiskell supported repeal of the Eighteenth Amendment as an abridgement of individual liberty, but refused to accept liquor advertising in the *Gazette* on the ground that he would thus be party to promoting sale of the stuff and he doubted that Arkansas had any conceivable need for an increase in consumption.

If a rigorous brand of Protestantism was the accepted order there was a remarkable incidence of dissent. Recalling her girlhood in the last century in a paper prepared for the Aesthetic

Club, an assemblage of Little Rock's most formidable matrons, Mrs. Hay Watson Smith wrote: "There were churches of course, and I went to one, but I cannot say it was much comfort to me. Besides the terrible hymns—'That awful day will surely come,' 'One more day's work for Jesus, one less of life for me,' 'When this poor, lisping, stammering tongue lies silent in the grave,'—there were sermons so full of the wrath of God that when I dreamed of falling . . . I was always falling into hell." [5] Entertaining such heretical notions apparently did not produce any kind of difficulty with this young lady's father, the estimable U. M. Rose, senior partner of the state's leading law firm. It may have strengthened her relationship with her husband, the Reverend Dr. Smith, a Presbyterian minister who won acquittal in a famous heresy trial before the Arkansas Synod and continued in his pulpit as one of the city's leading divines.

If Arkansans expected, and usually practiced, probity in the conduct of their ordinary affairs, they have, from the founding of the first government at Arkansas Post, displayed a pronounced tolerance for boodling by public officials. Roy Reed, one-time political writer for the *Gazette* who moved on to the *New York Times,* thought there was an inverse relationship between the almost Latin acceptance of political peccadilloes and the stringencies of the professed religion: "The Protestants, many of them barely two hundred years from the northern austerities of Scotland and Ulster and now Southerners through geographic happenstance, enjoy it as a forbidden fruit, as a country preacher enjoys sex." [6]

It was never possible to impose Victorian proprieties on the speech of ordinary Arkansans. The earthy tradition which accepts the bodily functions, sexual and otherwise, as interesting and frequently funny, could be more or less suppressed in formal mixed company, but it could never be eliminated in the ordinary discourse of the working day. For more than thirty years Vance Randolph fought a running battle with the university

5. *Arkansas Gazette,* Oct. 25, 1964.
6. Roy Reed, *New York Times,* Jan. 31, 1977.

presses that published his collected folklore but insisted that he bowdlerize the cruder Anglo-Saxon usage in the anecdotes of hill people. Randolph refused, contending that it would be truly obscene to substitute *penis* for *tallywhacker* in inditing a tale passed down across the generations. The level of obscenity and scatology now prevailing on college campuses finally emboldened the University of Illinois Press to bring forth a splendid collection of the material Randolph indignantly withheld from his earlier works. "It is impossible to present a well-rounded picture of Ozark folklore without some obscene items," he wrote in the introduction. "Such stories are not aphrodisiac, or intended to incite antisocial sex activity. They merely invoke laughter." [7]

Laughter may be the key to much that outsiders see as contradictory in the Arkansas style; I don't think the natives have ever taken their own cherished eccentricities as seriously as they have been taken by those who viewed them through a skewed cultural lens. In an admiring biography of J. William Fulbright, subtitled *Portrait of a Public Philosopher,* Tristram Coffin lapsed into what can only be described as reverse parochialism when he sought to contrast his subject—"a modern Prometheus, he defied the gods and myths of modern society to save men from the horror of atomic doom"—with the people from whom he sprang. Coffin depicted the Rhodes scholar errant coming home to seek approbation at the polls from the Arkansas Visigoths: "The Primitives, for their part, seem to be filled with a helpless choler against the Civilized Man like Fulbright. They are, crudely put, their betters. The Primitives are the mob ransacking the palace, not of anything of value but for the sheer physical pleasure of destroying treasures they could never possess." [8]

Fulbright testily rejected this kind of nonsense; the palace-wreckers with whom he contended were men like Joe Mc-

7. Vance Randolph, *Pissing in the Snow, and Other Ozark Folktales* (Urbana: University of Illinois Press, 1976), p. 4.
8. Tristram Coffin, *Senator Fulbright: Portrait of a Public Philosopher* (New York: E. P. Dutton & Co., 1966), p. 70.

Carthy, who came from progressive Wisconsin. When he finally was retired it was through an issue-free election in which Arkansas voters gently notified the old jouster that it was time to give a younger knight a chance at the dragons. Fulbright has since resorted to the *Columbia Journalism Review* to castigate those who perpetuated the myth of his philosophical divorcement from Arkansas:

> The sophisticated national press . . . has had a tendency to pose certain rather tedious "paradoxes" about my personality and my role. Is Fulbright truly a humanitarian idealist, or a racist under the skin? An "international peace prophet" . . . or "plain old Bill" regaling Arkansas rubes with talk about the price of cotton and chickens? How too, they have asked, anguishing on my behalf, can an "urbane internationalist" like Fulbright survive in a southern hillbilly state like Arkansas? But most of all my friends in the national press have pointed—more in sorrow than in anger—to the "paradox" of my "humanitarianism on a global scale" as against my early opposition to civil rights legislation.

Some of Fulbright's friends back home reacted more in anger than in sorrow when he decided at the outbreak of the Central High desegregation crisis to sit out the confrontation and continued to straddle the issue through his subsequent re-election campaigns. They, however, had no trouble understanding, and in the end accepting, at least the second half of his characteristically blunt explanation: "I did not vote for civil rights legislation prior to the late sixties for two very simple reasons: first, because I doubted its efficacy; second, because my constituents would not have tolerated it."

A politician who could remain in Congress from the early days of World War II until the end of the conflict in Vietnam, and in the course of that extraordinary epoch earn the plaudits of the civilized world, must qualify as an expert on the essential qualities of the electorate that kept him there. Bill Fulbright writes off the argument over "urbanity" and "provincialism" as "a conceit of the eastern 'establishment'." And we can, I think, close the case with his testimony that he did not find that "the representation in Congress of New York, Massachusetts, or California has been notably more responsible, intellectual, sophisticated, or humane than that of Arkansas. I have always felt attuned, responsive and at one with my home state." [9]

A student of the westward movement, Donald Atwell Zoll, contends that it produced a distinct "trans-Mississippi state of mind," which he describes as "the true flowering of the American Apollonian-Dionysian balance." [10] Arkansans would dismiss the characterization as highfalutin, but they would agree—indeed, insist—that the ancestral passage across the great river made them different. I found, living among them, that their ingrained southern gentility was undergirded by a sometimes splendid, sometimes destructive recalcitrance that appears to be a heritage from the impacted frontier. It will be the task of the author of the next chapter in the state's history to determine whether that quality can survive as the old isolation falls away and Arkansas belatedly enters the American mainstream.

9. J. William Fulbright, "Fulbright on the Press," *Columbia Journalism Review* 14 (November/December 1975): 43, 44.

10. Donald Atwell Zoll, "The Rise and Fall of the American Gentleman," *Modern Age* 20 (Spring 1976): 199.

Suggestions for Further Reading

The dedication of this book to Hugh B. Patterson, Jr., denotes not only my obligation to him, but to the institution he presides over as publisher of the *Arkansas Gazette*. The collection of rare books begun by J. N. Heiskell and now maintained by the newspaper has been mined by the curator, Margaret Ross, for her own indispensable work, *Arkansas Gazette: The Early Years 1819–66* (Little Rock: Arkansas Gazette Foundation, 1969). In addition she extracted from a wide variety of sources the "Chronicles of Arkansas" published in the newspaper over a period of years; these are scheduled to be collected in a single volume. Mrs. Ross's advice and guidance is reflected in whatever claim to factual accuracy may be made on behalf of the pre–World War I passages in my own work, although she bears no responsibility for the interpretations and conclusions.

There is no full-scale modern history of Arkansas. *Historic Arkansas,* by John L. Ferguson and J. H. Atkinson (Little Rock: Arkansas History Commission, 1966), a secondary school textbook, provides a sound but necessarily skeletal overview. John Gould Fletcher's *Arkansas* (Chapel Hill: University of North Carolina Press, 1947) is an eloquent impressionist account of the state's development, and the WPA Guide, *Arkansas* (New York: Hastings House, 1941) is still a valuable handbook. But both volumes run out at the point where Arkansas enters upon its great post–World War II transformation.

For the detailed record of the contemporary period I have relied primarily on newspaper accounts. Fortunately, I could call upon former colleagues at the *Gazette* who had firsthand knowledge of the major events; I am particularly indebted to Robert Douglas, Jerry Neil, Sam Harris, Leland DuVall, Charles Allbright, Tom Dearmore, and Betty Fulkerson.

I also have had access to the private libraries, and lively memories, of A. F. House, Esq., Edwin Eagle Dunaway, Fred K. Darragh, Jr., Mrs. James Vinson, the late Charlie May Fletcher, and the honorary sextons of Mount Holly Cemetery, Mrs. Booker Worthen and Mrs. George Rose Smith.

The major published sources are identified in the footnotes. Beyond these, I commend the *Arkansas Historical Quarterly* to anyone interested in the cultural aspects of the state's history. It is available in bound volumes in most of the state's libraries. Primary sources are available at the Arkansas History Commission.

Index